WHAT YOU SHOULD KNOW ABOUT
SUICIDE

BILL BLACKBURN

WHAT YOU SHOULD KNOW ABOUT SUICIDE

WORD PUBLISHING

Dallas · London · Vancouver · Melbourne

The Scripture quotation marked TEV is from the Today's English Version of the Bible, copyright © American Bible Society 1966, 1971, 1976.
Used by permission. Scripture quotations marked RSV are from the
Revised Standard Version of the Bible, copyright 1946, 1952, © 1971,
1973 by The Division of Christian Education of The National Council
of The Churches of Christ in the U.S.A., and used by permission.

ISBN 0-8499-3173-8 (pbk)
Library of Congress catalog card number: 82-050517

Printed in the United States of America
0 1 2 3 4 9 BKC 9 8 7 6 5 4 3 2 1

For
Pablo
with
remembrances of good times
respect
and
regret

Contents

Preface

On July 25, 1980, one of my closest friends committed suicide. When I received news of his death, I was not surprised, but I was saddened. Over a period of seven years he had contemplated suicide. Neither psychiatric help nor the support of family and friends prevented that death. My firm conviction, however, is that his death and many other suicides can be prevented—not all, but many. It is with this conviction that I write this book.

This volume proceeds from two basic assumptions. First, understanding suicide is a key to preventing it. Second, a close, open, personal relationship with the suicidal person is extremely important in preventing suicide. Therefore, my belief and prayer is that with this volume you will be a more informed, better equipped, and deeply committed helper in the fight against suicide.

The above paragraphs appeared in the preface of the first edition of this book which was published in 1982. Those two paragraphs tell you why I wrote the book and list its major assumptions. Now, eight years later, the reason for writing—suicide prevention—and the assumptions remain the same, but they are even stronger.

Because of this book and the attention it has received, I have gone from coast to coast to talk to school groups, ministers, counselors, and other groups. I have been on more than fifty radio and television shows. I have talked with suicidal persons, people who have attempted suicide, and family and friends of those who took their own lives.

Based on this contact with the problem, I am more convinced than ever that most suicides can be prevented and that informed, caring laypeople are crucial in this effort. Not only is that an assumption. It is a conviction born out of experience.

When I began writing the first edition of this book, I prayed that God would use it to help prevent suicides and the kind of pain I had seen my friend's death inflict on those who loved him. My prayer has been answered.

I have shared the information from this book in groups where someone began to realize that they had been seeing signs of suicide in a friend and had not recognized them as such. In more than one instance reported to me, the person's fears were confirmed, but when confronted, the suicidal individual in fact wanted help and received it. In Dallas, I was on a talk show dealing with suicide. A man walking through his living room with a bottle of pills, on his way to take them since his wife had just left him, heard what I was saying. I especially made a direct appeal to suicidal persons not to take their lives. He called a hotline number at the end of the show, got the help he needed, and came through that experience without the drastic "solution" he had contemplated.

I have been told by pastors, youth ministers, and counselors of times when the information in this book enabled them to intervene strategically in a suicidal crisis. With the numbers of volumes sold, the magazine articles adapted from it, and other ways this information has been disseminated, I am sure that many more accounts could be told of how God has used this volume.

But I would not want all of this talk of "success" to obscure the complexity and the perversity of suicide. Remember, I said most suicides can be prevented, but not all.

Some people are so intent on taking their lives that there is almost no way to stop them from doing so. And there are plenty of stories around of people knowledgeable about suicide who failed to see the suicidal symptoms of someone close to them. I emphasize this so that what is said in this book is put in the proper context. It is possible to prevent suicide, but realistically, a suicidal person can slip right past us to his self-chosen rendezvous with death.

The subject of suicide is so broad and there is so much information now available that I have chosen to limit my discussion to prevention and intervention. I deal very little here with post-suicide grief. When the book was first published I never envisioned that many who had lost a family member or friend by suicide would be helped by it. I have been surprised by the help it has been to many persons who have suffered this loss. But I want to reiterate that other books have been written specifically to help the person who has sustained this loss. These are listed in the bibliography at the back of this book.

The problem of suicide raises some important ethical issues. This, however, is not a textbook on ethics. I have assumed some things and left unaddressed others so that the exclusive focus of this book would be on prevention and intervention. This is not to say that the ethical issues raised by suicide should not be addressed. It is to say, instead, that the reader will need to look elsewhere for the philosophical debates about suicide.

How can you use this book? My intention is that in these pages you will find the help you need as you seek to aid a family member or friend facing the specter of suicide. Perhaps a suicide attempt has already been made or threats have been uttered. Someone close to you may already have taken his life. Alarm from news accounts may have prompted you to pick up this volume. Possibly your interest was sparked by the fact that you have an adolescent in your home, and you are concerned about the dramatic increase in the suicide rate among adolescents. Perhaps your husband or wife has shown signs of depression in recent days. For whatever reason you are now reading this, I believe that you will be helped by learning some of the reasons for suicides, clues to potential suicide, and specific ways to help and get help.

Two cautions should be raised here. What I have written is not intended to make you and will not make you a "junior psychiatrist" equipped alone to prevent someone from taking his life. People who care wisely—and communicate that care—are desperately needed by suicidal persons. But suicidal persons also need professional help. You are setting yourself up to fail if you single handedly take on the task of keeping a family member or friend from completing an act of self-destruction.

Second, this book is not intended as a preventive for persons who are themselves contemplating suicide. Probably some who read these words are now considering suicide. Although there may be some ways that this book might be helpful to you, through this book I cannot give you the kind of crucial help you need. I urge you immediately to seek professional help from a psychologist, psychiatrist, pastoral counselor, clinical social worker, marriage and family therapist, or a minister. If finances are a difficulty, help may be available through local churches, mental health centers, or suicide prevention centers. Reach out to someone *now*. Also, consider giving this book to your best friend or a close family member. It can help them to help you.

I would like to acknowledge some of the people who have aided me in writing and revising this book, but there are too many to mention all of them by name. They include my own family, friends, and fellow professionals. I am especially grateful to those persons whose lives have been marked by suicide and who shared, often painfully, about those experiences. They talked with me about sons, daughters, spouses, parents, friends, and themselves. Those who have shared so openly did so with the hope that they might prevent other suicides. I trust they did not share in vain.

On an editorial note, for clarity and consistency, throughout the book I have used masculine pronouns where the reference was to either male or female. I originally sought to use both "he" and "she" and found this style to be confusing and cumbersome.

Now I invite you, the reader, on a journey of learning. In a sense, you will become a student of suicide. Learn from the reality of suicide in our culture the *who* and the *why* of suicide. Learn to see the signs and how to help and how to understand your own feelings and sense of responsibility in the face of suicide. Why do you become this kind of student to learn these kinds of things? I assume you do so because you care, and because you want to help someone who is now on the road to suicide.

WHAT YOU SHOULD KNOW ABOUT SUICIDE

1

Why Do People Take Their Lives?

MANY CANNOT conceive how people could come to the place of taking their lives. The question "Why?" looms large in the face of suicide. As in most other instances, though, in the case of suicide the answer to why is an elusive and complex commodity. Perhaps three examples of suicide and attempted suicide will help illustrate the elusiveness and complexity of this question.

Example One

Although not the most popular boy on campus, Michael had a number of close friends and found great satisfaction in sports activities. During the ninth grade, though, a bout with hepatitis kept Michael out of sports for most of the year. In the summer before he was to enter high school, Michael's father, an electrical engineer, was promoted and transferred to another state. In August the family moved to their new home, and Michael was two weeks away from entering a new school. Because of eligibility requirements and some lingering physical problems, it would now be another year before Michael could participate in sports again.

As school started, things seemed to be going well for the family. Michael's father was busy getting established in his new job, his mother was busy getting acquainted in the community

3

and was already involved in activities at church. Michael's only brother had left for his junior year at college.

What was not noticed immediately was that Michael was becoming increasingly withdrawn and seemed to talk of few new friends at school. He complained a lot about being tired. When Michael wrote his brother and mentioned that he wanted him to have his album collection, the brother became alarmed and called his father about his concern.

That night Michael's parents began to probe sensitively and carefully about how things were going with Michael. They discovered that he had moved quietly into depression and had started skipping classes at school. To their dismay, he told them he had even considered using one of his father's guns to kill himself.

Michael and his parents soon began seeing a family therapist and on holidays the older brother joined them for several sessions with the therapist. Some lingering difficulties were dealt with in the family and Michael began specific steps to build his support system of friends at school. At last report, the prognosis for Michael was good.

Example Two

With vague and uncertain career goals, Cindy completed the spring semester of college. She had decided to go to summer school to pick up some extra courses and so she could remain at school to be with Robert, her boyfriend since March. In early June, Robert told her that he would be dating some other girls that summer but would "try to see her as much as he could."

Since her parents' divorce when she was eighteen, two years before, Robert had been the only boy Cindy had dated regularly, and she had begun to think about the time they might get married.

Cindy was devastated by Robert's announcement about dating around. After two days of little sleep, no food, and much crying, Cindy called Robert to ask him to come to her apartment that night.

What resulted was a shouting and crying fight with Cindy threatening to take her life. Robert finally left with nothing resolved. Cindy took a bottle of tranquilizers from her medicine cabinet, swallowed them all in one gulp, and lay down on her bed.

After driving around for about an hour, Robert went back

to the apartment. Alarmed when Cindy did not answer his knock, Robert raced down to get the apartment manager. They got into the apartment, found Cindy semiconscious, and rushed her to the hospital, where the emergency room staff pumped her stomach, provided other medical aid, and admitted her to the hospital.

After a stay of a week in the hospital that included a psychiatric consultation, Cindy went back home to spend the summer with her mother. She did not see Robert again.

About six weeks after getting out of the hospital, Cindy again attempted suicide. This time she was admitted to a psychiatric hospital. Cindy is presently getting the intensive help she needs and seems to be improving.

Example Three

James, a twenty-nine-year-old owner of a small heating and air-conditioning company, faced possible bankruptcy. After high school he had gone to work for a large heating and air-conditioning firm. He had learned quickly and had become a skilled technician. He chafed under the limitations of working for someone else and especially was angered by his demanding, cocky supervisor.

At twenty-seven James had saved enough money to start his own business. His wife, who had been working elsewhere, was now able to be at home with their two preschool daughters while she did bookkeeping and telephone relaying for the company.

Plagued by bad business decisions, a sluggish economy, heavy competition, and poor help, the company faced rough times from the start. James, with every setback, pushed himself more feverishly. No stranger to hard work, since his father had died when he was three and he had worked what seemed like all of his life, James began keeping longer hours, beginning earlier every day and staying later almost every night. With the business finally reduced to one other employee, he was having to work on almost every job himself. Cautioned to slow down, James pushed even harder.

The dream began to crumble. There seemed to be no hope of salvaging the business. On Monday, James stayed home all day. He was tired and worn out. He did some work on Tuesday and a little more on Wednesday. On Thursday he sent word by a friend that he was resigning as a deacon at his church because of "personal reasons." On Friday, unknown to his wife, he took out additional life insurance on himself and spent the day getting business affairs in order.

The weekend was spent with the family, and James seemed more relaxed and at peace with himself. Sunday was spent at church and watching football, with dinner out with all the family that evening. On Monday morning, after lingering a while after breakfast, he hugged and kissed his wife and both of the girls.

James drove in his pickup to a narrow rural road outside of town. At what was estimated to be seventy-five miles an hour, James ran head-on into a large oak tree. He was killed immediately. A "psychological autopsy" done at the request of the life insurance company established the cause of death as suicide. This verdict was upheld in court, and the proceeds from the insurance policy were denied the family.

How would you answer the question, "Why did these three persons attempt or complete suicide?" In Michael's case, was it due to the move, his illness, his social isolation, or inattention from his family? With Cindy, was it solely because of Robert or did it have something to do with her general uncertainty about her life goals? Was her parents' divorce a factor? In James's case, the precipitating event seemed to be the failure of his business; were there other factors?

In each of these cases, as we shall see later, there were certain conditions present that along with other factors and the turn of events were predictors of possible suicide. One of the main goals of this book is to enable you to be alert to those clues. But even those clues do not fully answer the question *why*.

In truth, people attempt or complete suicide for a variety of reasons. In each attempted or completed suicide there are usually several, if not many, reasons for the action. In an effort to understand the suicidal person better, an examination of some of those reasons can be helpful.

In this chapter we will look at those internal motivations for suicide, the reasons suicidal persons themselves report in the notes they leave or in conversations following an unsuccessful attempt at suicide. In the sixth chapter, "Who Is Responsible?," we will examine such factors as genetics, biochemistry, family tendencies, and the situational environment.

If we could peer into the mind of the person contemplating

suicide, one of the overriding emotions we would see would be ambivalence. The desire to live and the desire to die exist side by side; these desires are engaged in a powerful struggle. At one stage of the process those conflicting wishes are expressed in a resigned attitude of indifference, "I don't care if I live or die."

If this tug of war between life and death were not present, why would Marilyn Monroe be found dead clutching the telephone? Why would Sylvia Plath, the poet, be found with a note asking that her medical doctor be called? Why would a person, as has often been the case, drive up to the emergency room of a hospital and then shoot himself? In what are strangely humorous occurrences, why would a potential suicide obey when a policeman rushes into the room with pistol drawn and orders him to drop his gun? In one instance a man jumped off the Brooklyn Bridge in New York City and refused to grab a life preserver thrown to him. A policeman from the bridge shouted, "Grab that life preserver or I'll shoot!" The man grabbed the life preserver and was pulled to shore. Ambivalence reigns.

Suicide is a gamble. Many suicidal persons are very conscious of the risk factor and are tempting fate to see if life or death will win out. One writer has likened this gamble to the romantic game of pulling petals off a flower. "Life loves me, life loves me not." In some instances, God is being tempted. "I am going to try to take my life, and if You really love me, You'll see to it that I'm not successful."

I emphasize this aspect of ambivalence because too often persons see the suicide attempt only as a "gesture" and therefore conclude the person was not serious. Even in the "gesture," however, some desire to die is present. On the other hand, when a person completes suicide, there is commonly the failure to see that he wanted not only to die, but also to live.

Yet there are persons who seem to have no ambivalence about their suicide. They seem only to want to die, and there is virtually no way to prevent their death. Psychiatrists and hospital personnel have many stories to tell about the persons who have, after every means of killing themselves had been removed, still found ways to self-destruct. These persons had one goal only and that was to take their own lives. But I assert that it is a small minority of suicide attempters and completers who merely want to die. The remainder want both to live and to die.

Every suicide is an attempt to say something. What and to whom are important clues to understanding suicide.

Motivations for Suicide

In the following pages we will consider some of the motivations of persons who attempt or complete suicide.[1] Realize that for many persons there would be a combination of several of these factors.

1. To escape from an intolerable situation

Most suicidal persons want to escape from what they consider an intolerable situation. The shape of that situation varies with each individual, and many other persons in similar situations do not consider suicide an option. Two important ingredients for those who begin to ponder taking their lives are hopelessness and faulty reasoning. These two are linked: there seems to be no hope of resolving the situation, but the reason hope does not appear is that the suicidal person is not thinking carefully or clearly. Sometimes this is because of mental illness. In any event, this is a frustrating thing for persons working with suicidal individuals. The hope that may be obvious to another, the suicidal person does not see.

2. To punish the survivors

Suicide is almost always a hostile act. Often the hostility of the act is directed toward the survivors. This is a form of the child's retort, "I'll die and you'll be sorry." In fact, one school of psychotherapy maintains that the person who takes his life is fulfilling a childhood vow in which he has said, "If it ever gets bad enough, I can kill myself."

As we shall see in more depth later, important questions to ask a suicidal person are, "Who will find your body?" and "What effect will your death have on those closest to you?" To know who will find the body may answer the question of whom the person is most angry with, although that is by no means always the case. In response to the second question, there is sometimes a slight hint of a smile as the individual thinks of the grief that will be caused by his death.

One young man who took his life did so just as his parents had left for a needed and faraway vacation. On their second day away, they got the news of their son's death. A teenage girl took her life on the afternoon of the night her parents were to celebrate her father's promotion to the presidency of a small manufacturing company. Frequently suicide is attempted or completed after a mate has announced his or her intention to divorce or after the divorce has been finalized. Somewhere along the way either the husband or wife has made the threat, "You'll be sorry for this."

Suicide or attempted suicide can be a powerful way to punish the survivors. Sometimes that desire to punish overrides the desire to live.

3. To gain attention

A suicide attempt grabs attention like few other actions. People are startled, guilty, concerned, puzzled. Where people previously ignored a person, now they lavish attention on him. This flurry of attention and concern lasts for only a season and then things return to normal. To regain attention, another suicide attempt may be made. This pattern may be repeated many times.

Does the person who is seeking attention really want to kill himself? The answer, as for almost all suicidal persons, is probably yes and no. In a life in which suicide attempts seem to be the only or the best way to gain attention and "love," the person is living a fairly bare existence and death may seem preferable to life. Even though such persons may actually prefer to live rather than die, once a suicide attempt has been made, suicide becomes for them a more attractive option.

Should a person who seems only to be seeking attention be taken seriously when he makes a suicide attempt? Yes. Any person who talks about, threatens, or attempts suicide should be taken seriously. For one thing, some people have attempted suicide in a way they thought would not succeed, and it did. Second, when someone has become so desperate as to gain attention by a suicide attempt, that person needs serious help in learning to cope and to gain perspective. Third, many of these attention-seekers keep attempting suicide and increasing the lethality of their methods until they finally succeed. It could be argued that they still did not mean to kill themselves, but they had to increase the intensity of their attempts to be taken seriously. Finally, the danger was so great they completed what they had attempted before only for effect.

4. To manipulate others

Although akin to efforts to gain attention, this reason for attempting suicide is designed to get more than attention. There is a specific object or action the person is seeking. The desire is to elicit a response that seems otherwise unattainable. A suicide attempt can be the trump card played after all the other cards have been played.

Manipulation by attempted suicide is used by children against parents, husbands against wives, girlfriends against boyfriends, workers against co-workers.

More will be mentioned later about how to deal with this kind of attempt, but again it must be stressed that this person should be taken seriously. By taking him seriously, I do not mean that you should acquiesce to his demands to keep him from killing himself, but you should get help in dealing with the potential of suicide because the threats do become real and the manipulators do succeed sometimes in taking their lives.

5. To join a deceased loved one

To be reunited with one you love by following him through the door of death is one of the most ancient and persistent motives for suicide. The anxiety of separation and the desire to be present together in the "peaceful" state of death moves many from suicidal thoughts to suicidal actions.

In many cultures there are or have been elaborate rituals centered on the death of a person about to be joined again with his or her beloved deceased one. The Hindu ritual of suttee called for the widow to sacrifice herself on her husband's funeral pyre. In the Japanese culture, Junshi is a form of suicide for those who wish to join a leader or master in death. Shinju, practiced by the lower classes, is a form of double suicide so the "lovesick" can be joined in death.

Though not ritualized in our society, this is still a compelling motive for many suicidal persons. Surely this is one reason for the high rate of suicide among older persons in the United States. But this motive is by no means limited to the older population.

Sylvia Plath, the American poet who took her life while living in England in 1963, had earlier written in her poem "Daddy,"[2]

> At twenty I tried to die
> and get back, back, back to you.
> I thought even the bones would do.

Her father had died when she was nine, but the idea of rejoining him persisted with her for twenty-one years.

Careful attention needs to be paid to a child's or adolescent's view of death lest he innocently or impulsively attempt suicide following the death of someone he loves.

6. To avoid punishment

Why would anyone take his life rather than face punishment? What can be worse punishment than death? Remember that the suicidal person is usually not thinking rationally, and also death is, to some, preferable to the form their punishment will take.

The frequently reported suicides in jails and prisons are often motivated by a desire to avoid punishment although the punishment has already started.

An example of this kind of motive can be seen in the life of a young bookkeeper we will call James. He had served one tour of combat duty in Vietnam in 1970. Upon returning to his hometown, he entered the local junior college and began taking courses without really knowing what he wanted to do following graduation. He began dating a girl, Tammy, from a nearby small community. Sensing the seriousness of their relationship, Tammy's father began talking with James about his career goals. Recognizing James's good math abilities, he began to talk to him about the field of accounting.

After dating for almost a year, James and Tammy married, and through Tammy's father's influence, James landed a job as bookkeeper in a small, locally owned manufacturing firm. James and Tammy quickly became overextended financially. The financial problem was compounded when the couple learned that they were expecting their first child.

With a private and serious commitment to repay all he "borrowed," James began to juggle the books at work in order to have enough to make ends meet. As is so often the case, nothing was paid back and the sum "borrowed" grew at a steady rate. After two years of this, James was discovered when he was absent one day. The employee who filled in for him noticed some irregularities and reported them to the office manager, who promptly went to the owner of the company.

As the news began to spread, James's despondency and shame grew. His father-in-law was horrified, his fellow employees surprised, and his wife saddened but compassionate. As the extent of his crime became known and as James faced up to the reality of an almost certain prison sentence, despondency turned into despair. Suicidal thoughts went from occasional to continual.

Through a previous experience with attempted suicide in another community, a local pastor who had some contact with the family took the initiative to visit James at his home. When the pastor asked if he had given thought to suicide, James seemed relieved to talk about a plan of suicide he had devised. The dominant motivation seemed to be an avoidance of punishment. The thought of going through a public trial and then being separated from his family while in prison was almost more than James could bear. Through a coordination of efforts with the local authorities and later the prison officials, and through continued contact with the pastor, James received the kind of help that gave him enough hope not to attempt suicide.

Though certainly also motivated by guilt and shame, James was among that number of persons who consider death by suicide preferable to the impending punishment.

7. To be punished

For some, suicide is a self-inflicted form of punishment. Self-destruction is always a form of punishment, but it is not always the chief motivation behind the act.

Sometimes a disturbed understanding of God contributes to this motivation of seeking punishment. This can be seen in persons who feel they have committed the "unpardonable sin" and therefore must be punished. There are some who feel that since they have committed this unforgivable sin and will burn in hell for it, they might as well end their lives rather than live on in a miserable existence. Interestingly and sadly, persons who reach this disturbed state of mind consider their particular "pet sin" to be the unpardonable sin, whether that sin be masturbation, lust, "evil thoughts," or taking the Lord's name in vain. According to Scripture, the unpardonable sin is the hardened resistance to the convicting work of the Holy Spirit that leads to salvation. Essentially, this sin is the refusal of salvation. For a person who becomes convinced that he deserves damnation because of the "unpardonable sin," usually no amount of Scripture teaching or discussion of doctrine will help. When a person comes to this point, professional help is needed to bring him out of his confusion.

Though it is certainly a manifestation of mental illness, there are some people who come to feel that they are Satan reincarnated or that Satan dwells in them. Therefore, to kill themselves is to rid the world of Satan.

Apart from such confused religious understanding is the victim-induced homicide. This is essentially the form of suicide in which the person wants to be killed but sets someone else up to do the killing. Most often the victim provokes the police to kill him by endangering the life of others or the police. Although the victim-induced suicide is not always an attempt to be punished, it is that when the person has committed some crime for which he feels he needs to be punished. Some persons even commit crimes that normally get the sentence of death in order to let the justice system do their suicide for them. These victim-induced suicides differ from martyrdom-seeking suicides. In the latter, death is to advance some cause; in the former, death is sought simply for itself.

8. To avoid becoming a "burden"

In an act of what they often consider genuine love, some people destroy themselves so they will not become or continue to be a problem or burden to those around them. This motivation is often associated with such debilitating and frequently fatal diseases as cancer, Alzheimer's disease, or multiple sclerosis.

Suicide notes reveal this motivation sometimes in cases of alcoholism or mental illness. Though these diseases may not be fatal, when the person sees no hope for improvement and only envisions being a continuing problem to the family, he may decide suicide is the best way out. This same motivation may occasionally be seen where a person has respectability and status in a community, and he becomes involved in a scandal that may be followed by a trial and much public attention. To avoid the embarrassment to everyone, suicide may be attempted.

Tragically, this motivation is also present in the case of an unwanted child or a child whom the parents grow to dislike and wish they did not have. Sometimes these feelings of the parents are verbally expressed to the child, but even when they are not, the child senses the feelings. With a defiant child, the reaction may be anger and antisocial behavior. With a compliant child, though, this motivation to comply may be mixed with a motivation to punish the parents by his suicide.

9. To avoid the effects of a dreaded disease

This reason is akin to the above, but the difference is sometimes almost indistinguishable because the person is essentially seeking to spare himself the suffering and slow demise of a dreaded disease. Further, it is an attempt to control the time that the death will occur.

Among adolescents, a debilitating illness, even though it may not be fatal, may precipitate a suicidal crisis. This seems to be more acute among adolescent males than females.

Though pregnancy is not classified as a dreaded disease, it may be seen as that by a young unmarried woman. Because of the availability of abortion and the increased acceptability of single women bearing children, suicide among pregnant, unmarried young women is not as prevalent today as in the past. Pregnancy out of wedlock may still be the primary factor in some suicides, though.

10. To pursue an irrational, impulsive whim

As do other motivations for suicide, this one appears strange and almost unbelievable. A small number of suicides, however, can be attributed to what seems an unpremeditated, impulsive act.

Adolescence and young adulthood are times of experimentation and exploration. There is a fascination with the untried and

the unfamiliar. Death seems so remote and
invulnerable to it that they are drawn to expe
through drugs, guns, or automobiles. Sometin
are fatal. Included in this would be drug ov
such as Russian roulette and forms of "chicker

In many such cases the death can be clas
intentioned death." Though there was not   ious, deliberate seeking of death, there was an almost unconscious,
half-hoped-for death. Janis Joplin, the rock singer who died
from an overdose of drugs, was remembered by some of her
friends as playing delightedly with death even as far back as high
school days.

Sometimes, on careful examination, the person who seems
to have committed suicide on an impulsive whim actually had
courted death for years.

11. To seek martyrdom

Many martyrs seek their martyrdom. Others have it thrust
upon them, sometimes unwittingly. How, though, can seeking
martyrdom be a form of suicide? It can be simply because the
death is anticipated and chosen even if it is carried out by others.

The earliest Christian teachings against suicide arose in part
because so many Christians were seeking martyrdom at the
hands of the Romans. Augustine, the Bishop of Hippo, in writing
against suicide, borrowed from Plato's *Phaedo* some of his arguments against suicide. Augustine also argued against suicide on
the theological premise that life is a gift from God and therefore
should be treasured and not destroyed. Through Augustine we
inherit the erroneous notion that suicide is an unpardonable sin
which means that all persons who take their lives will be eternally damned.

Obviously, in our society, with the freedoms we enjoy and the
basically nonviolent political traditions that are ours, there are
fewer opportunities for martyrdom than would be the case in
other times or in other societies.

To some individuals, part of the attraction of being a dead
hero is that in death they may know a fame and honor they did
not know in life. Abdul, an Iranian student in the United States,
had earlier become famous in his own country when it was

...ieved that he had been killed by the dreaded state police. His picture appeared everywhere in public places and his name became a rallying cry. With some dismay he let it be known that he was still alive. Almost to avoid the embarrassment, he came to the United States as a college student.

Death haunted Abdul. When he had been thought dead, he was a hero. Alive, he was rather ordinary. Suicide became a way he could return to the days of fame. He made several unsuccessful attempts, then finally took his life when his American girlfriend broke up with him. Even under these circumstances, Abdul returned to Iran something of a hero as an indirect casualty of the hated Shah's regime. A taste of martyrdom left an unfulfilled hunger. Like other martyrs before him, however, Abdul failed to heed the words of Albert Camus from *The Fall:* "Martyrs, *cher ami,* must choose between being forgotten, mocked, or made use of. As for being understood—never!"[3]

12. To express love

Though akin to other reasons listed above, this reason is present so often that it deserves special attention.

Following the breakup of a romance or marriage, a suicide may also be a tragic way of letting the other person know just how much he or she was loved. Even after the death of a mate, this motive may sometimes drive a person to suicide. In a distorted and confused way, the survivor thinks only this drastic action will communicate to the world how strong the love for the deceased mate was.

A friend of mine going through divorce described how he became suicidal when he thought about not being married and not living with his children. He was not sure the marriage should continue, but the thought of being a divorced father was so disturbing that to be dead seemed a better alternative.

This same phenomenon is present in some murder/suicide cases or joint suicides. The thought of living without each other is so strong that both partners decide to walk the path together to death, thus reenacting the sad story of Romeo and Juliet.

Tragically, some romantic partners and some children feel this is the only way they can adequately express their loyalty to their dead loved one.

The Factor of Mental Illness

Many of the above reasons listed for suicide or attempted suicide seem rather rational and deliberately chosen. Though that is not in fact the case in all these instances, it does raise one other question: What about mental illness as a cause of suicide?

Some contend that every person who attempts or completes suicide is mentally ill. Only a mentally ill person would want to take such a drastic measure to deal with a problem, they insist. Also, these persons argue that anyone who is so depressed that he wants to take his life must be mentally ill.

Almost all careful students of suicide, however, claim that not all persons who attempt or complete suicide are mentally ill. Though the estimates vary, only about one-third of the people who complete suicide attempts could be described as suffering from mental illness.[4] The other two-thirds certainly might have benefited from some form of psychotherapy, but they could not be classified as mentally ill.

Among people who are suicidal, depression is the most common diagnosis of mental illness. Depression diagnosed as resulting from factors in the person (endogenous depression) rather than factors in the environment (exogenous or reactive depression) is the mental disorder with the highest suicidal risk.[5] Among adults, manic-depressive psychosis is specifically the most common diagnosis among suicidal persons, with the suicide attempt occurring in the depressive phase. Manic-depressive psychosis is characterized by alternating mood swings from energetic elation to lethargic hopelessness.

Among suicidal young persons who are diagnosed as mentally ill, schizophrenia seems to be the most common diagnosis. Since about two-thirds of all schizophrenics enter the early phases of their illness in adolescence and since the majority of schizophrenic suicides occur early in the illness, it is not difficult to see why this diagnosis is common among suicidal adolescents with mental disorders. More will be mentioned later about understanding the symptoms of schizophrenia.

Many times, following a suicide, the family members will attribute the suicide to mental illness even when there is no clinical evidence to support that assertion. Sometimes the family is right. But other times this seems to be the best strategy they have in coping with the death. If the suicide can be attributed to mental illness, alcoholism, or the abuse of other drugs, then it seems to the family and others that the person was not responsible or at least not completely responsible for his action. In other words, the contributing agent, mental illness or drug abuse, becomes the villain, and the person becomes a hapless victim.

Though this may be some help in coping with a suicide or suicide attempt, it denies the reality of the person's responsibility for his actions, however that responsibility was impaired by other factors. As Erwin Stengel has said, "Motiveless suicide does not exist even in psychotic mental disorders."[6]

What Does the Bible Say about Suicide?

The Bible reports seven suicides. They are described with little comment and without condemnation. The biblical basis for making a case against suicide comes not from these seven incidents but from the broader understanding of life as a gift from God. Murder is wrong, even taking one's own life.

The seven suicides in the Bible are these:

1. *Abimelech* (Judges 9:50–55). Abimelech was the ruthless, immoral son of the Old Testament leader Gideon. He ruled Israel for three years following the death of his father. In the siege of the city of Thebez, Abimelech's skull was cracked when a woman dropped a large rock on his head as he approached the city's tower. Rather than suffer what he perceived to be the shame of dying at the hand of a woman, Abimelech called on his armor-bearer to "run him through" with his sword.

2. *Samson* (Judges 16:23–31). Samson was leader of Israel during the time of the Judges. He was known for his physical strength, but his moral stamina did not equal his physical prowess. Finally captured and blinded by his archenemies, the Philistines, Samson asked God for strength just one more time that he might bring revenge on his captors. As the Philistines mocked Samson and rejoiced in high spirits, Samson pushed out the two main pillars of the Philistine temple and ended his own life along with the lives of several thousand Philistines.

3. *Saul* (1 Samuel 31:1–6; 1 Chronicles 10:1–14). Saul was the first king of Israel. His reign was at first blessed of God, but then he became increasingly disobedient and "the hand of God left

him." In a fierce fight with the Philistines, Saul was critically wounded and his three sons killed. Saul asked his armor-bearer to kill him with the sword. The armor-bearer refused, so King Saul took his own sword and fell on it.

4. *Saul's armor-bearer* (1 Samuel 31:1–6; 1 Chronicles 10:1–14). When Saul's armor-bearer saw his master and king dead, he followed him in death in the same manner.

5. *Ahithophel* (2 Samuel 17:24). Ahithophel was a trusted advisor to King David, but when David's son Absalom mutinied against his father, Ahithophel became one of Absalom's advisors. However, Ahithophel, whose advice the scripture declares "was like that of one who inquires of God," became dejected when his advice was not taken. He went to his hometown of Giloh, set his house in order, and then hanged himself.

6. *Zimri* (1 Kings 16:8–20). Zimri was an advisor to Asa the king of Judah, but in the twenty-seventh year of Asa's reign, Zimri killed the king and succeeded his monarch on the throne. After only seven days as king of Judah, Zimri had to fight off the forces of Omri who were seeking to avenge the death of King Asa. When Zimri saw that his defeat was at hand, he entered the royal palace at Tirzah where only the week before he had killed Asa. Zimri set fire to the palace, thus ending his own life. The Bible notes that he died "because of the sins he had committed."

7. *Judas* (Matthew 27:5; Acts 1:18). Judas was one of Jesus' twelve disciples. As is well known, Judas betrayed Jesus in the end. After Jesus' arrest, Judas repented of what he had done and tried to return the money he had received for the betrayal. "Then," as the Bible notes, "he went away and hanged himself."

So, what were the methods and the motives of these seven suicides recorded in the Bible? Three (Abimelech, Saul, and Saul's armor-bearer) died by the sword. One (Samson) died when he pulled down the Philistine temple. Two (Ahithophel and Judas) hanged themselves. One (Zimri) died in a fire he himself set.

As for motives, three (Abimelech, Saul, and Zimri) took their lives in the face of approaching and certain death. Samson's motive was revenge. We can assume Saul's armor-bearer died at his own hand because of grief or fear. Ahithophel and Judas took their own lives because of remorse and dejection.

As noted earlier, these seven suicides are recorded in scripture with little comment or commendation. But looking at them together, if a summary were written of each of these lives, it could be written in bold letters: T–R–A–G–E–D–Y.

Conclusion

Why do people take their lives? For all the reasons listed above, for more, and for combinations of all of these. The motivations for suicide are usually more complex than simple. Why people destroy themselves takes us to both the trivial and the profound, the simplicity of life and the mystery of life, the transparency of some persons and the opaqueness of others.

Suicide seems to raise more questions than it answers, but in the chapters ahead some of those questions will be addressed.

2

Can Suicide Be Prevented?

APPROXIMATELY THREE-FOURTHS of all suicides can be prevented. Yes, the implication of that statement is that some suicides are virtually unpreventable. But this whole book and an entire international movement is based on the firm belief that most suicides can be prevented. They can be if there are informed people who care enough to risk becoming involved in the lives of other people who are or may become suicidal.

Consider the case of Robert, a thirty-one-year-old new-car salesman. When he came to work at a new-car dealership in a large southern city, he began as a service writer in the service department. Because of his appealing way with people, his outgoing personality, and his desire for advancement, he caught the eye of the sales manager. When the sales manager approached him about becoming a new-car salesman, the opportunity seemed just what he needed since sales were then good and his growing family was requiring more income than he was making. He accepted the offer.

In the first two years on his new job, things went well, with Robert moving steadily up the sales ladder and a number of times leading the other salesmen in monthly sales. He seemed to have it made. But then economic recession hit and sales of domestic new cars plummeted. There was even talk of the dealership going out of business. At home, Robert and Jeanie now had three children;

the oldest was seven and the youngest, three. With the income continuing to lag behind, some bills were going unpaid, and it looked as if Jeanie would have to go back to work outside the home. Other factors were also causing the marriage to be unsatisfying for both of them.

Robert began to show up later and later for work, and his old "spark" just was not there. Two of his best friends had already left the company for other work, and he missed their support.

Robert's sales manager, Walter, a veteran car salesman in his fifties, became concerned about Robert—as a person, not just for his performance. Five years before, a friend of Walter's had committed suicide. Following that death, Walter had entered the volunteer program of the local suicide prevention center. Through the training he received there and from his years of manning the telephone crisis line at the center, he recognized the symptoms of a potential suicide crisis with Robert.

Late one afternoon, he asked Robert to go out for a cup of coffee with him. At the coffee shop, Walter told Robert some of the things he had been noticing. He asked him, "How bad has your depression gotten?"

"Pretty bad," Robert replied, after a long sigh.

"Has it gotten so bad you've thought about taking your life?"

Looking up as if to say, "Can I really trust you?" Robert said, "Yeah."

"When's the last time you thought seriously about it?"

"I think about it all the time now."

"How would you do it?"

"With a gun."

"Do you have a gun?"

"Yeah."

"Where?"

"In the car."

After a lot more talking, Robert agreed to do three things: to give his gun to Walter, to see a psychiatrist Walter recommended, and to allow Walter to call one of Robert's closest friends about what was happening. But perhaps most important, Robert had now talked about his suicidal thoughts to someone who genuinely cared and who exhibited that care.

Robert did see the psychiatrist and began taking a mild antidepressant. He and Jeanie soon began marital therapy with a clinical social worker on the psychiatrist's staff.

The suicide crisis passed. Robert eventually had to move to another job, but he still stays in touch with his friend Walter. Jeanie began working outside the home, and though there are still some difficulties in the marriage, at least they do not seem as overwhelming as they once did.

What happened here? Put simply, one person was hurting and another was willing to listen to that hurt and take some steps to help—the Good Samaritan revisited.

An important factor here is that Walter had some information that helped him care appropriately. He was the beneficiary of a movement that is relatively new.

The Movement to Prevent Suicide

As the professions devoted to helping others have developed, their practitioners have tended to follow the example of their forebears, medical doctors, by seeking ways to help people who are in a crisis and need immediate assistance. Therefore, psychologists, social workers, and pastoral counselors for years for the most part dealt with people who came to them bearing the signs of a crisis. Medical doctors continued in the same way.

In the twentieth century, and especially in the last forty years, a revolution has been occurring that is transforming the way all the helping professions see their work. The prevention of crises rather than simply the handling of crises has come to the fore as an important and possible task. Whether in medicine, psychology, dentistry, nursing, social work, pastoral counseling, or marriage and family therapy, the terms *prevention, enrichment,* and *wellness* are heard more frequently. A part of the whole move toward lifelong learning in the form of continuing education is based on the theory that certain crises in people's lives can either be avoided or dealt with more adequately if people have the right information and skills.

In 1958, in the field of suicide prevention, two Los Angeles psychologists, Norman Farberow and Edwin Shneidman, with a grant from the National Institute for Mental Health, established the Los Angeles Suicide Prevention Center. This center was a harbinger of things to come in the field of suicide prevention.

At about the same time that Farberow and Shneidman were doing their pioneering work in Los Angeles, an organization called the Samaritans was formed in England for the purpose of helping persons who were suicidal. The Samaritans began using what was then a revolutionary approach by utilizing unpaid lay volunteers as crisis counselors. This approach came to be a crucial element among suicide prevention centers in the United States.

At a national conference on the study of suicide in 1968, the American Association of Suicidology was formed to promote research and public education about crisis intervention and suicide. The organization continues to pursue these goals through an annual meeting, the publication of a journal, and by serving as the certification agency of crisis centers. Today there are over seven hundred suicide prevention centers in the United States.

Now the crucial question: Has this movement toward suicide prevention decreased the number or rate of suicides in the nation? The answer is a qualified no. In the United States the number of suicides and the rate continues to be high. Among certain groups, such as adolescents, young adults, and black males, the rate has dramatically increased.

Can it be concluded, then, that suicide prevention is a failure? No, because many suicides have been, are, and will be prevented by suicide prevention centers and other forms of suicide prevention. But given the turbulence of the last thirty years, the moral and social revolution that has been occurring, the increased abuse of alcohol and other drugs, the increased number and availability of handguns, and many other factors, it is little wonder the suicide rate has increased. That rate could very well be beyond where it is today if the efforts toward suicide prevention of the last three decades had not been made.

We are increasing our knowledge of suicide every day, and the methods and forms of suicide prevention are being refined, but without further public awareness of the causes of suicide and the basics of suicide prevention, the battle against suicide cannot be adequately waged.

What Do the Statistics Tell Us?

Technically, statistics do not tell us anything. They simply are there, and we draw certain conclusions from them. Where suicide is concerned, drawing conclusions from the statistics can be risky business. First, it is difficult to determine at times just how accurate the statistics are. Many deaths that are suicides do not get recorded as that either because the death is not clearly a suicide or it is covered up in order not to lose insurance benefits, or to keep from embarrassing the family. Second, we do not have a long history of accurate statistics on suicide. It is difficult to compare what we are now discovering about suicide with earlier times, even the last century. Third, depending on the sources quoted, suicide statistics can vary rather considerably. In this book, where I have found statistics that vary significantly, I have generally used the more conservative figure.

Another reason why drawing conclusions from statistics about suicide is risky is that statistics can seem to be cold and hard and unreal compared with the living reality of loved ones who may be in danger of taking their lives. We want to say, "But we're talking about people, not statistics!" That is true, and where it is appropriate to use statistics, I have tried to do so sensitively rather than cavalierly. The fact is, we need good information about suicide to understand it better. To the degree that our actions are based on good information we are able to be more effective helpers. Because statistics provide information that helps us to be more informed helpers, let us see what they have to "tell" us.

The "typical" suicidal person

The "typical" completer of suicide in the United States is an older white male. The "typical" attempter of suicide is an adolescent white female. The attempters may eventually be completers of suicide because about 45 percent of all persons who take their lives have previously attempted suicide. Females attempt suicide three times as often as males, but males complete suicide three times as often as females. The male-to-female ratio, in other words, is three to one of completed suicides. In part this difference can be accounted for by the methods chosen. Women tend to use slower-acting, less lethal methods such as drugs and gas. Men tend to use faster, more lethal methods such as guns, cars, and hanging. That is beginning to change, however, as the "democratization" of suicide occurs and more women become completers of suicide. The year 1978 was the first in U.S. history when more women used guns in taking their lives than drugs.

Age and sex

Statistics reveal that the longer a man lives the greater will be the chance he will take his own life. In fact, the highest rate of suicide occurs among white males age eighty-five and above. In contrast to the overall rate for American males, among nonwhite males there is a peak of suicides at about twenty-five years of age with a decline to age forty-five and then a series of rises with a peak at about seventy-five years of age.

For American women the rate of completed suicides peaks between forty-five and sixty-five years of age. The nonwhite female population has the lowest suicide rate with a peak at age thirty-two after which there is a gradual decline except for a rise at about age forty-two.

Marital status

Generally, suicide occurs less frequently among married persons than among single people. Suicide rates are higher among never-married persons and widowed individuals and highest among the divorced. Among married persons under twenty-four years of age, however, the suicide rate is higher than for singles. It has been conjectured that many of these persons sought marriage as a solution to problems and when that did not solve all their problems, suicide was tried.

Time of year and week

The lowest month for the number of suicides seems to be December. Though depression and loneliness can be acute during the holiday season, there is apparently enough excitement and contact with family and friends to keep the suicide rate down.

The months with the highest number of suicides are April and May. Some surmise that as the earth springs to life after the deadness of winter, the sadness and hopelessness of the suicidal person become even more poignant as he contrasts his own inner state with the aliveness of his surroundings.

In general, suicides are most likely to occur on a Friday or a Monday. However, among African Americans the majority of suicides occur on Wednesday.

Social conditions

The suicide rate is higher during times of national economic stress and lower during times of war. The highest suicide rate in

U.S. history (17.4 per 100,000) occurred in 1932 at the height of the Depression.

Why is the suicide rate lower during times of war? Suicide is an act of aggression. War involves acts of aggression against others, the enemy. Our tendency is not to be aggressive against ourselves when we are moving in aggression against another. The British suicidologist Erwin Stengel notes, "The invariable decline of suicide during war is probably due to a change in the balance of aggression."[1]

Geography

For years the Rocky Mountain and Western states have led the nation in the highest rates of suicide. For the most recent year's statistics available at this writing, the highest states were as follows:

Rank-State	Rate (per 100,000 pop.)
1. Nevada	24.1
2. Montana	21.7
3. New Mexico	19.4
4. Arizona	19.3
5. Wyoming	19.1
6. Idaho	17.7
7. Colorado	17.6
8. Oregon	16.7
9. Florida	16.0
10. Washington	15.3

In the same year, the lowest states were:

50. New York	7.6
50. New Jersey	7.6
49. Massachusetts	9.2
48. Connecticut	9.6
47. Rhode Island	10.2
45. Hawaii	10.8
45. North Dakota	10.8
44. Illinois	11.0
42. Mississippi	11.1
41. South Carolina	11.4[2]

Internationally, the countries with high suicide rates and the ones with low rates usually stay about the same. For instance, the rates are generally low in Australia (11.8), the Netherlands (11.2), Scotland (10.9), New Zealand (11.2), Portugal (9.4), England and Wales (8.6), Italy (7.3), and Spain (4.8). The rates are consistently high in some countries. In recent years, the highest rates were in the following:

Hungary	44.1
Denmark	26.9
Austria	26.7
Finland	26.3
Belgium	22.7
France	21.8
Switzerland	21.4
Japan	21.1[3]

There is much speculation about why certain regions of the United States and the same nations are consistently high. The reasons include such factors as alcoholism, availability of firearms, religious beliefs, social customs, climate, economic/social conditions, and accuracy of reporting.

High-risk groups[4]

There are certain high-risk groups in our society that are particularly vulnerable to choosing suicide. The groups listed here represent some of the most clearly identified high-risk groups.

1. Elderly white males. This group has the highest suicide rate of any group in the United States.

2. American Indians. The suicide rate on some reservations is five times the national average. Their highest suicide rates occur among persons between the ages of fourteen and twenty-five and are closely related to alcohol abuse.

3. Physicians. The number of physician suicides in one year equals the number of yearly graduates from the average size American medical school. The average age for a physician who takes his life is forty-eight to forty-nine. He usually has graduated from one of the better medical schools, tends to be perfectionistic, often has a poor marriage, and frequently is an abuser of alcohol and/or other drugs.

4. Adolescents. In recent years suicide has been either the second or third leading cause of death among adolescents. The rate of suicide among adolescents has risen alarmingly over the last several decades.

5. College students. Suicide is the second leading cause of death among college students. Accidents are first.

6. Alcoholics. It is estimated that 20 percent of the people who take their lives are alcoholics, with another 20 percent problem drinkers. Therefore, alcohol is related to almost half of all suicides.

7. Drug addicts. Although it is often difficult to determine if a death due to drug overdose is a suicide, suicide among drug addicts and users is high.

8. Homosexuals. Though suicides are high among homosexuals, not enough research has been done to understand fully this phenomenon. With the onset of the AIDS epidemic, however, the rate of suicide among homosexuals has increased.

9. Unemployed men. A number of studies have shown the correlation between unemployment among males and suicide.

Though technically not a high-risk group, children five to fourteen years of age are not immune to the lure of suicide. The suicide rate for this group has almost doubled in the last decade.

Fables and Facts about Suicide

There is much misinformation about suicide. We will be helped by examining the fables and the facts of suicide since many people who are confronted with a suicidal person attempt to prevent that suicide while operating with erroneous notions.

1. Fable: People who talk about suicide won't do it.

Fact: It is estimated that about 80 percent of persons who take their own lives have given signals about their intentions. Suicide threats should always be taken seriously.

2. Fable: Mentioning suicide may give the person the idea.

Fact: For a person who is considering suicide, having someone to talk the idea out with can be a powerful preventive. If the person has not thought about suicide but is obviously anxious or depressed, to talk about suicide not being a good option can be a preventive measure. You can assume, though, that most depressed or very anxious persons have given some thought to taking their lives.

There are some situations, however, that raising the issue of suicide may be better done in a veiled way rather than directly. With some persons, I do not use the word suicide, but will ask such questions as, "Have you gotten so down, you have thought about harming yourself?" "Have you gone so far as to think about doing something stupid?"

3. Fable: Suicide occurs without warning.

Fact: Suicide is the result of a process that in retrospect can be traced back sometimes for years. Almost always the suicidal person plans how he will take his life and then gives clues to his intentions.

4. Fable: All suicidal persons are mentally ill.

Fact: Although the suicidal person may be unhappy, anxious, and upset, not all persons who take their lives could be diagnosed as mentally ill.

5. Fable: The tendency toward suicide is inherited.

Fact: There is debate about this one. There now seems to be some evidence that there are genetic factors which result in a proclivity toward suicide in some families. (See Chapter Six for more information on this.) Even apart from genetic factors, when suicide occurs in a family, that increases the chances for suicide among the rest of the family. In other words, this has been a fable that seems to contain some fact.

6. Fable: Once people are suicidal, they always will be, and they are beyond help.

Fact: The suicidal crisis is generally of a brief duration and if intervention and therapy occur, the person may never again seriously contemplate suicide. It is true, however, that about 10 percent of the persons who attempt suicide eventually take their lives. (A clarification may need to be made here. Of all people who attempt suicide, only 10 percent complete suicide. On the other hand, of all people who complete suicide, about 45 percent had previously attempted suicide.)

7. Fable: Suicidal persons are completely committed to dying.
Fact: The dominant feeling of most suicidal persons is ambivalence. They want to die, but they also want to live.

8. Fable: It is not a suicide if there is no note.
Fact: Only about one-third of the persons who take their lives leave a suicide note.

9. Fable: When a depression lifts, the suicide crisis is over.
Fact: The greatest danger of suicide occurs in the first three months following a deep depression. The happiness and peace of mind exhibited by some persons as they come out of a depression actually result from the fact that they have finally "resolved" their crisis by deciding to take their lives.

10. Fable: The poor and the rich are the most likely to destroy themselves.
Fact: Suicide crosses all socioeconomic boundaries, and no one group has a proportionately higher incidence than another.

11. Fable: People who are alcoholics do not usually commit suicide.
Fact: There is a very high correlation between alcoholism and suicide, with an estimated one-fifth of all alcoholics ending their lives by suicide. Many people who are not alcoholics drink heavily prior to killing themselves.

12. Fable: Suicidal people do not seek out medical help.
Fact: Several studies have indicated that as many as 75 percent of persons who take their lives visited a physician within three months prior to the suicide.

13. Fable: Professional people do not commit suicide.
Fact: There are high suicide rates among physicians, dentists, pharmacists, and lawyers. Contrary to another fable, dentists *do not* have the highest suicide rate among professionals.

14. Fable: December has the highest suicide rate of any month.
Fact: December has the lowest rate. April and May have the highest rates.

15. Fable: Suicide is the unpardonable sin.

Fact: Though this has been taught by various groups within the church, it is based on the notion that sins have to be forgiven prior to death or to be expressed to people before death. The unpardonable sin, though, is the refusal to yield to the convicting work of the Holy Spirit which leads to salvation. So, in essence, the unpardonable sin is the refusal of the gift of salvation.

Conclusion

Can suicide be prevented? Yes, and part of our attempt to prevent suicide is through an accurate understanding of suicide. Now that we have spent two chapters on understanding suicide, it is time to examine the specific signs to look for as predictors of a possible suicide crisis.

3

What Signs Should I Look For?

SOME OF THE MOST knowledgeable people in the field of suicide prevention maintain that 80 percent of all persons who take their own lives give clues as to their intention. If that is so, and I believe it is, then a significant step is taken toward suicide prevention when we learn the signs pointing to suicidal risk.

In discussing these signs, however, it must be recognized that the presence of a single sign may mean little. When, though, there are a number of indicators, a "cluster of clues," careful attention should be given to the possibility of suicide.

This emphasis on looking for a number of clues rather than only one or two is important because with the knowledge gained from this chapter, you can run the risk of becoming a junior detective ready to jump to conclusions when the evidence does not warrant it.

During the late sixties, in response to the widespread abuse of drugs, many parents became involved in drug-education seminars that included information about spotting drug abuse. Two of the most common signs the parents were told to look out for were redness of eyes and sniffling. Many a teenager was pounced upon with a barrage of questions when, in fact, he or she was only suffering from hay fever!

Having warned you against jumping to conclusions, let me now warn you against denying what you suspect. If you sense some signs of suicide, without prying or being obtrusive, check out what you suspect. A good motto is, "When in doubt, check it out." You may do so with a few questions, or you may choose to talk to others who have been with this person—teachers, co-workers, friends, family, and others.

Because suicide is such a drastic measure, our natural inclination is to say, "Oh, he wouldn't do that!" The reality is that he may. We also have an inclination to tell ourselves, "She's just not the type to do that!" Any "type" may come to a place of considering suicide.

After the suicide of her close friend, a woman told me, "For years I'd seen the signs, but I kept ignoring them. Why? I guess because I never wanted to believe it. And how do you say to someone, 'You're acting crazy'?"

There is one "type" of person who may be very adept at concealing his intentions, but there is every evidence that this is exactly the kind of person in whom people deny seeing any thoughts of suicide. This is the attractive, bright, promising, "together" person. When this kind of person commits suicide, the common response is, "He is the last one I would have suspected of that." Denial of the signs may be a very great risk for parents because, where there are high expectations of a child, it is so unthinkable to entertain any notions that the child might kill himself.

I am, of course, asking you to walk a tightrope between being overanxious about seeing signs of suicide and denying the signs you suspect. This is not an easy task, but it is an important one. For me, I would rather fail at this task on the side of caution than on the side of denial.

To aid you in recognizing the signs of suicide, I have divided them into four categories—stress factors, personal history, behavioral clues, and verbal clues. After reading this chapter, you will be better able to answer the question, "What signs should I look for?"

Stress Factors

Every person experiences stress. In fact, the absence of stress is harmful. Hans Selye, the Swiss pioneer in the study of stress, has made a helpful distinction between stress and distress.[1] Not all stress is bad, but for a variety of reasons stress can become distress.

In understanding the possibility of suicide in the face of stress, it is crucial to be able to distinguish between stress and distress as evidenced in the response the person makes to the stress. When you note that the coping abilities of a person under stress are beginning to fail, you should know that the possibility of suicide is increased. Coping means simply handling adequately the situation at hand. Coping includes maintaining equilibrium and perspective. Many persons experience several stressful events and still maintain their "copability." Other persons, given the same circumstances, may find themselves exhausted in trying to cope. Once exhausted, they are tempted to give up. One form of giving up is suicide.

The signs of this breakdown in coping ability are (1) either outward signs of inability to cope or a perception on the person's part that he cannot cope, (2) severely limited perceptions of himself and his difficulties, and (3) acute ambivalence about dying and living and receiving help.[2]

In simpler terms, a breakdown in coping ability can be described as a feeling of *helplessness.* The person feels he has exhausted his options to handle the situation and is therefore helpless. Combine this feeling of helplessness with a feeling of *hopelessness,* and the risk of suicide may be at its greatest. Aaron T. Beck, a psychiatrist specializing in the treatment of depression, has led his colleagues in testing psychometrically and clinically Beck's thesis that hopelessness is the key variable linking depression to suicidal behavior. In this state of hopelessness, the person exhibits "impaired reasoning" because every avenue he examines as a way out of his situation seems to him to lead to a negative conclusion. To avoid suicide, the hopelessness must be dealt with.[3]

In the face of all this, you may be asking, "What kind of stressful events occur that test a person's ability to cope this severely?" Stressful events include everything from death of a mate to a new job, from being fired to having a child, from illness to inheriting a large sum of money. In the pairs of instances mentioned here, the latter might hardly be seen as stressful, but in reality even the good things of life can be stressful. Given this diversity, how can we sort out stressful events that might be signs of suicidal behavior?

Stressful life events can be divided into seven categories. With each of these seven categories, I will note some examples of suicidal behavior.

1. Loss of relationship

The loss of a relationship is stressful, whether that loss comes through death, divorce, desertion, institutionalization, moving, or through some other way. Obviously, the closer the relationship, the more stressful the loss will be. But some teenage fans have even taken their lives after the deaths of rock stars, sometimes in the same way the star died. Sadly, a few children have taken their lives after the death of a pet. With these teenagers and children, previous signs of isolation and romantic notions of death seem to have been dominant.

But no loss of relationship should be taken lightly, especially not with children or adolescents. The "puppy love" of early or later adolescence is taken with utmost seriousness by the lovers and the end of that relationship may seem to them to be the end of everything.

Certainly the loss of a mate through death or divorce is stressful, but again the most important question is the response of the persons coping with the stress and whether they perceive themselves as coping.

Until recently, little attention was paid to the stress experienced by children of divorce. Often, to avoid inducing further guilt, people will tell divorcing parents, "The kids will cope. Kids are more flexible than we think." The reality is that we are just now beginning to understand how devastating divorce can be for children. In one study of suicide attempts by forty adolescents, divorce had occurred among 32 percent of the adolescents' families.[4] The divorced parent need not feel helpless about the situation, however. It should be noted that the manner in which the divorce is handled, and especially the child's awareness of love and protection from the parents, are crucial in helping him cope with the divorce. When love is present and expressed, when communication lines remain open, and when both parents remain involved with the child, the stress of divorce is lessened for the child.

The loss of a relationship in and of itself is no sign of suicide, but it is a stressful event that should be taken seriously by the persons close to the one who has suffered the loss. As can be seen from the above examples, the most important question to be asked is, "What does this loss mean to this person?"

2. A major blow to the ego

Certainly the loss of a relationship can be a blow to the ego, but in this section of our discussion we are referring to blows to the ego that do not technically involve loss of relationship.

Unemployment is one such blow to the ego. To be fired or to be laid off, even for good reasons, can result in a significant loss of self-esteem. It is no accident that the suicide rate reaches its highest point during times of economic recession and depression. Not to have work and thereby not to have the means to provide for oneself and one's family can result in tremendous feelings of remorse and hopelessness. Also, with unemployment, a suicide may be a way of telling the former employers, "You'll be sorry for this."

Though not seen by our society as the "tragedy" it was formerly perceived to be, pregnancy out of wedlock is no less a stressful life event. Especially for the young teenager, this event can be so stressful that ending one's life may seem the course to take. This is especially true in very rigid homes where the teenager perceives that she will meet with nothing but rejection and hostility.

Pregnancy out of wedlock always raises the question of abortion, and it should be noted that some persons have taken their lives following an abortion. In almost all cases, the woman had received inadequate or no counseling, and the guilt and remorse combined with the bodily reaction were so great that suicide seemed warranted.

On the opposite side of a blow to the ego by an unwanted pregnancy is the loss of a wanted, unborn child. Though this is in a sense a loss of a relationship, I am including it here because the reaction that may lead to suicidal behavior is the loss of self-esteem felt by many women following a miscarriage or a stillbirth. The loss of a child, especially if it is not the first such loss and there are not other children in the home, can lead to feelings of inadequacy, self-doubt, and guilt. A friend of mine who had finally conceived after much difficulty and a long wait, had a miscarriage early in the pregnancy. Though she could not explain why, shame was her most dominant emotion. Through a strong marital relationship and with the help of a sensitive gynecologist, suicidal behavior in such situations can be detected and deterred.

Losses to the ego could also include such events as physical impairment, failure in business or school, rejection by significant others, or retirement.

3. Prolonged illness with pain

Since this kind of event is so evident and specific, little time will be spent explaining it. It needs to be noted, however, that we should not assume just because the person has coped with such a situation for months or even years that he or she will continue to do so, given only the prospect of the continuation of the limitations and pain.

4. A developmental barrier

Only in this century have we begun to understand more fully the developmental process of human beings, and only recently has major attention been paid to the adult's developmental process. However we number the stages or conceptualize them, they are no less important in understanding human behavior.

When there is a barrier to our development as persons, there will be stress. Whether it is the teenager who is unable to make friends of either sex, the college student adrift in vocational indecision, the young wife and mother terribly dissatisfied with her life, the middle-aged woman depressed by a sense of futility, or the retiree unsure of what to do with himself, there will be stress.

Though actually not a developmental barrier, some children are so pushed to succeed and advance to the next "stage," they become depressed and even suicidal because they feel they are not advancing fast enough. Such a child David Elkind has called the "hurried child." These children are victims of our hurry-up, success-oriented society. The famous pioneer in the field of child development, Jean Piaget, was once lecturing in the United States. Following his presentation of the child's developmental states, a father asked, "Is there a way to speed up this process?" Piaget replied, "Only in America would I be asked that question. I can't imagine why you would want to speed up the process."

One particularly painful developmental barrier that plagues many late adolescents and young adults is what is termed "homosexual panic." In developing their understanding of their sexuality many persons at this age question whether or not they are homosexual. Even if they are not, they may convince themselves that they are. And for most homosexuals the realization of their sexual orientation creates high anxiety and often depression. Whether it is an unfounded panic or a growing awareness of their homosexual tendencies, for no small number, suicidal behavior is evident at this stage. Since this kind of struggle can be so private and so concealed, it may seem that this is hardly a sign which can be seen. In fact, though, most persons in this stage will begin asking questions, however indirect, that may give the watchful observer clues to rising anxiety or even suicidal thoughts. Even beyond this, good sex education should include accurate information about homosexuality, including the fact that for all but a small percentage of persons a homosexual orientation is in no way inevitable or irreversible.

In all cases of stress due to developmental barriers, the important question is, "What are the dreams of this person, how are they blocked, and what does that blockage mean to them?"

5. Self-imposed high expectations

Perfectionism carries with it its own stress. Being mortals who have failed, who now fail, and who will fail, when we set our sights on perfection we set ourselves up to guarantee our sense of failure.

The perfectionist can never fully relax because he always has much left yet to be done before perfection is attained. Neither can he enjoy his accomplishments because they are tarnished by their lack of perfection.

A clinical social worker who works with emotionally disturbed children and adolescents and their families noted one common denominator among all the children and adolescents she saw who had attempted or completed suicide. Each was very self-punitive. They punished themselves severely because of their "failures." This self-punitiveness, so frequently a part of perfectionism, leads to a degree of self-loathing that is a precursor to suicide.

In his book on suicide, *The Savage God,* the British literary critic A. Alvarez comments on the perfectionist who seeks to end his life:

The psychoanalysts have suggested that a man may destroy himself not because he wants to die, but because there is a single aspect of himself which he cannot tolerate. A suicide of this order is a perfectionist. The flaws in his nature exacerbate him like some secret itch he cannot get at.[5]

The tragedy is that the perfectionist does things so well that when he attempts suicide, he generally succeeds.

6. Mental illness

Mental illness takes many forms, all stressful. For our purposes, I will discuss only two forms of mental illness, depression and schizophrenia. Realize, however, that any form of mental illness is a stressor and merits careful attention lest the possibility of suicide be overlooked.

How does one distinguish between the "low" feelings that all of us experience and depression? Basically one does this through understanding the person's view of the future. Depression is characterized by pessimism. The depressed person is not just sad; he is convinced that his sickness will be with him no matter what he does.

Why do people become depressed? For some, depression is a response to a specific event like the loss of a loved one. For others, depression seems to occur without a direct cause. The former type of depression is called reactive or exogenous and the latter is called endogenous. The person with endogenous depression is simply more prone to the problem and is susceptible to periodic bouts with it. Though there is the danger of suicide occurring in a reactive depression, generally the risk is higher with the endogenous form.

Whatever the type of depression, we are helped by understanding its signs. Most lists include the following common signs:

(1) Sleeplessness or excessive sleeping. Difficulty falling asleep and especially early morning waking accompanied by anxious thoughts are signs of depression. Excessive sleeping can be a sign of depression.

(2) Loss of appetite or excessive eating. The loss of interest in eating may also be accompanied by a loss of interest in sexual activity.

(3) Languor. Loss of ambition, interest, and ability to concentrate. With the depressed person, there is little sense of aliveness. The lack of ability to concentrate may be seen as an intense concentration on something that is simply an escape from reality. One friend, whose husband took his life, told me of how, in the days prior to his suicide, her husband spent hours playing a tabletop baseball game.

(4) Guilt or discouragement. There is the presence of self-remorse, hopelessness, and self-deprecation.

When all four of these factors are present, the risk of suicidal behavior is high.

An important distinction should be made here between adult depression and adolescent depression. Drs. Frank B. Minirth and Paul D. Meier, two Christian psychiatrists who specialize in the treatment of depression, note that whereas adults look and act depressed, adolescents often present depression in an atypical manner. Minirth and Meier observe, "Instead of looking and acting depressed, they may act out their depression. Very moral, conscientious teenagers may begin to steal, to lie, to take illegal drugs, or to misbehave sexually as a result of being depressed emotionally."[6]

In her book on depression in women, Maggie Scarf notes another sign of depression among adolescent females. That sign is an "accidental" pregnancy. Often this can be a desperate attempt to deal with feelings of being unwanted and unloved. The teenage girl fantasizes "lavishing upon *her own baby* the tenderness and nurturance for which she herself so longs and aches."[7] In another place, Scarf calls such an "accidental" pregnancy "getting company inside one's skin."[8]

In regard to the second mental illness related to suicide, schizophrenia is such a complex and confusing phenomenon that it seems almost ludicrous to discuss it in a few short paragraphs. Its relation to suicide, however, compels us to do so.

In an article entitled "Conditions Predisposing to Suicide," C. P. Miles estimates that 10 percent of schizophrenics ultimately die by suicide, approximately 3,800 each year in the United States.[9]

Contrary to the commonly held belief, schizophrenia is not split or multiple personality. Schizophrenia is a mental disorder that includes severe disturbances in perception, thought, emotion, and mood, resulting in irrational behavior. Schizophrenia takes a number of forms, including simple, hebephrenic, catatonic, and paranoid.

Though there is considerable debate about the incidence of suicide among schizophrenics, it concerns us here because many of the unexpected and mysterious suicides of young people may be attributable to schizophrenia. The onset of schizophrenia is generally in the adolescent or young adult years. As Max Day and Elvin V. Semrad point out in *The Harvard Guide to Modern Psychiatry,* "When onset is acute, the patient is faced with three alternatives for dealing with his unbearable pain: homicide, suicide, or psychosis."[10]

In a helpful little booklet on schizophrenia, Arthur Henley lists some prominent signs of schizophrenia:

1. Marked changes in personality.
2. Crying jags that defy rational explanation.
3. Loss of self-confidence, self-reliance, or self-esteem.
4. A constant feeling of being watched.
5. Difficulty in controlling one's thoughts.
6. Severe depression without real reason for it.
7. Growing edginess, tension, and unexplainable fear.
8. A sharp slump in academic or job performance.
9. Increasing withdrawal from people.
10. Excesses such as overcleanliness, food faddism, and compulsive religiosity.
11. Hearing voices.
12. Abrupt and unexplainable changes of plans or job.
13. Regular headaches and insomnia.[11]

It should be obvious that none of these signs by themselves or even several together necessarily indicates schizophrenia, but when there is a possibility, a competent psychiatrist trained in psychiatric diagnosis should be consulted early.

As I indicated in the preface, this book is not intended to make you a junior psychiatrist, but I hope the above information concerning two forms of mental illness will help to make you a more informed front-line helper.

7. Success

Success would hardly seem to be a sign of stress. Some successes, though, do generate considerable stress. The stress comes from trying to adjust to the new circumstances occasioned by the success, feelings of being overwhelmed and inadequate, and feelings of frustration because the success did not bring the much-hoped-for fulfillment and meaning.

Roger was thirty-seven years old when he was promoted to the head of his department over several older employees who had been with the company longer. Because he was aware that he had been promoted above some of his fellow-workers, Roger assumed his new responsibilities with some feelings of guilt. He also began to feel woefully inadequate for the task. The amount of work seemed overwhelming and the stress involved was more than he imagined. Soon he was working late every day, going to the office on weekends, skipping lunch, and seldom getting away for any recreation.

The downward spiral of guilt, stress, and feelings of inadequacy seemed to have Roger in its grip. In this confused state, for the first time in his life, he began to think he would be better off dead. An alert co-worker, one of the older men Roger passed on the way up the ladder of success, sensed what was going on and stepped in with some needed support, advice, and perspective. Because he stepped in early and because of Roger's resiliency, a tragedy was averted. Success demands its price.

Success is such an idol in our society that some have come to invest it with magic powers. "If only I could succeed in reaching my goal," they say, "then everything would be beautiful." When the goal is reached, though, many of those same people begin to ask, "Is this all there is?" A sense of futility and hopelessness sets in.

Whatever form the success takes, whether it is a job promotion, graduation, or the birth of a child, remember that, contrary to our normal expectations, success can be taking its toll.

Personal History

Knowing the personal history of a person can give you significant clues as to the possibility of suicide. Granted, there are some people who take their lives whose history would not indicate any signs of suicide. But as we will explain here, there are factors in the lives of some people that raise some red flags of warning.

1. A previous attempt

Of persons who complete suicide, about 45 percent have attempted previously (although of all persons who *attempt* suicide, only about 10 percent go on to *complete* suicide). Therefore, knowing that a person has previously attempted suicide should significantly increase the suspicion that under considerable stress this person will at least seriously consider suicide.

Realize that the large majority of people who attempt suicide do not go on eventually to take their lives. So it cannot be said that someone who attempts will inevitably later complete suicide, but it is important to note the percentage of persons who complete suicide who had attempted previously.

Part of the difficulty with persons who make several attempts is that their attempts are taken less and less seriously. They have cried "Wolf!" too often, and their attempts are passed off as attention-getting ploys. They may be like Cindy who at twenty-one took her life after three previous attempts and left a note that in part said, "You would not believe me. I was serious. See?"

2. The death trend

For some years now researchers in the study of suicide have found what has come to be termed the "death trend" among people who attempt or complete suicide. The death trend refers to the high incidence among suicidal persons of the loss by death of a significant person, especially before the suicidal person entered the adult years.

In an article contained in the book *Clues to Suicide,* two physicians, Leonard M. Moss and Donald M. Hamilton, reported that in 95 percent of the cases they studied the death trend was present. This involved the "death or loss under dramatic and often tragic circumstances of individuals closely related to the patient, generally parents, siblings, and mates."[12] In 75 percent of the cases, the deaths had occurred prior to the patient's completion of adolescence and in the other 25 percent, the death trend occurred later but was a precipitating factor in the person's becoming suicidal.

Though this study is now more than twenty-five years old, the death trend has continued to be shown to be a very important factor in predicting suicide. Obviously not all persons who lose a family member early in life later attempt suicide. Why, for some, does this seem to be a precursor of later problems? One important factor seems to be the disruption caused by the death. If the death resulted in significant changes in the sense of support felt from the rest of the family, economic status, living conditions, or other such factors, these changes seem to increase the chances of trouble later on.

As might be expected, the presence of suicide in the family is a significant factor in the death trend. Some studies have indicated that the child of a person who completed suicide is from six to nine times more likely to take his own life. Other studies of hospitalized psychiatric patients who committed suicide found that as many as one-third of the patients had in their family histories suicides that had had a dynamic impact upon them.

Suicide has a ripple effect. Sometimes these ripples become tidal waves that inundate the family and others close by.

3. A history of depression

Because depression has been dealt with earlier in this chapter, I will not elaborate here on depression as a personal history clue to suicide. Suffice it to say that a long history of depression or depressive episodes further increases the chances of suicide.

4. A history of being abused as a child

Because violence is early introduced to the abused child as a way of dealing with frustrations, it is hardly surprising to learn that some studies indicate that abused children have a higher rate of suicide.[13]

Further study needs to be done to understand the different suicide rates among physically abused, sexually abused, emotionally abused, and neglected children.

Behavioral Clues

"Listen to the language of behavior." That is good advice whether it is given to parents, teachers, counselors, or other friends. Behavior speaks volumes to us about what is happening to another, if we will just listen. Listening to the language of behavior is strategic in detecting suicide.

Attention will be given here to six types of behavioral clues that signal a possible suicide.

1. Preparing for death

Though some people simply decide it is prudent to "get things in order" for death, others begin preparing for death as a way of sending signals that they are about to end their lives. These preparations for death may include drawing up wills, increasing insurance coverage, planning a funeral, inquiring about how one donates his body to a medical school, giving away valued possessions, resigning from clubs and organizations, and making large contributions to charitable organizations. If these preparations are noted, further inquiry needs to be made about what these preparations mean.

2. Getting a means to attempt suicide

If a person who has never owned a gun in his life suddenly decides to buy one, that may signal some suicidal thoughts. A person's urgent plea to his doctor for sleeping pills or "nerve pills" may be a way of seeking the means to end his life. The same would be true if a family member begins inquiring about the medication in the family medicine cabinet and what each medication does.

If a person who never drinks alcoholic beverages or someone who never drinks to excess makes a sudden change in his drinking habits, he may be using this way of gaining "strength" to take his life.

3. Isolation, withdrawal

Too often people pass out of our daily lives and it is only weeks or months later that we realize they have been gone. Even in the intimacy of a family, sometimes silence and withdrawal go unnoticed. Wayne Oates includes the silence of a seemingly happy child as one of the "silences you cannot safely ignore." He notes, "The 'good child' is not necessarily at peace or happy."[14]

How do you respond when someone close withdraws? Do you first think that you might have done something to hurt or make them angry? At what point do you move past fear to find out what is really happening? Oates describes our possible response if we fear our now-quiet friend is on the path to suicide:

> Something is going on which you cannot quite put into words. The silence perturbs you. It creates a noise in your heart. At the very least, you can stay with and be with the person as much as possible. At the most, you can see to it with all the urgency with which you would respond to a high fever, that he or she gets to a doctor. Your attention to the silence is the thing that makes you special to the person.[15]

Attention to silence, isolation, and withdrawal is a guard against having someone drop out of our lives only to learn later of their suicide or attempted suicide.

Simple indications of withdrawal often are signs that all is not well. A business partner who stops eating with colleagues, a person who spends excessive amounts of time alone at the office or at home, or a person who fails to respond to social invitations may be indicating unhealthy isolation.

Obviously, when we are separated by distance from a family member or friend, sensing isolation may be more difficult. For a college student away at school, a young adult living in another city, or a relative recently living alone following the death of a mate, telephone contact plus correspondence and occasional visits will maintain his contact with us. But attention should also be paid to the level of emotional support where he is. When no friends are mentioned, no activities described, and no outings related, then further inquiry about isolation may need to be made. Simply to raise the question, "Are you finding yourself pretty lonely these days?" may help you sense what is really happening.

4. Consulting a physician

There are some indications that as many as three-fourths of all people who attempt suicide have seen a physician within the last three months prior to the attempt. This is another of those cases in which this sign alone should not be overemphasized, but when it is present with other signs of suicidal behavior it can be significant. For instance, in a study done in Oxford by K. Hawton and colleagues, it was found that 50 percent of adolescent self-poisoners had seen their physician within one month and 25 percent within one week of attempting suicide.[16]

M. Miller drew a profile of the "typical" male suicide using interviews with the widows of 30 men who completed suicide in Maricopa County, Arizona. One of the significant variables found indicating suicidal intent was a visit to the physician within a month prior to death.[17]

5. A suicide note

The leaving of a suicide note is such a clear indicator of suicide that it seems no one would ignore it. Unfortunately, some do. Either it is dismissed as just a ploy or an irrational whim or the person who wrote the note is confronted and denies he was serious or just laughs it off as a joke. Do not be put off by such lame explanations from a person who has left a note where it can be found stating he plans to take his life.

6. Sudden changes in behavior

When the tightwad begins to spend excessively, the normally quiet person talks incessantly, the depressed person suddenly becomes better, the highly moral person begins to act immorally, the person always careful of appearance begins to appear disheveled, some flags of concern and caution ought to go up. What's behind this sudden change?

Often it is nothing more than a brief aberration or a desired change in the routine. Sometimes, though, it is a clue that something is wrong. Again, this clue in the absence of others should not be weighted too heavily, but it ought at least to be put on the scales to see how it balances out.

One such clue that should never be ignored is crying on the part of a person who is never seen to cry. This is a sign of genuine and deep hurt that needs attention.

Verbal Clues

A forty-five-year-old mid-level manager, whom we will call Robert, almost casually remarked to a fellow office worker, "John, if anything ever happens to me, would you please clean out my desk for me? There are a few things there that I wouldn't want some people to see." A few weeks later, late in the day, the same two men were visiting before leaving for work. John asked, "How about stopping off at the club downstairs before we head home?" Robert replied, "No, I need to stay here and clean some things out of my desk." That night Robert took his life.

Should John have picked up on these verbal clues? Why didn't he? The chances are that it never occurred to him that Robert might take his life. Only in retrospect did he understand the signals Robert was giving him.

My hope is that as you read these pages, your alertness to such verbal clues will be significantly increased, for what often seems to be an innocuous statement is actually a signal for help.

The kinds of verbal clues to watch for include the following:

"I've had it."
"I'm through."
"I've lived long enough."
"I'm calling it quits—living is useless."
"There's a better way."
"I hate my life. I hate everyone, everything."
"It was good at times, and I can't complain, but we must all say goodbye."
"Now they won't have me to kick around anymore."
"I won't need another appointment, doctor. Don't take it as an insult. You were very helpful."
"Do you believe in reincarnation?"
"I'd like to come back someday. Maybe things will be better then."
"If I don't see you again, thanks for everything."
"I'll be back to haunt them all."
"Really, you won't have to worry about me anymore—that's for sure."
"I have a premonition—I'm going far away on a long trip."
"What's wrong with cremation?"
"I've been seriously thinking of making out my will."
"Do you know the procedure for donating your eyes after death?"
"How do they preserve kidneys for transplantation if you die suddenly?"
"I wish I could tell you how important you've been. You've helped me to see things clearly. Now I know the only road that's open for me."
"Life is like a short circuit. There's a sputter, then the lights go out."[18]

Other verbal clues include:

"I'm not the man I used to be."
"My family would be better off without me."
"Life has lost its meaning for me."
"Here, take _____ (valued possession) since I won't be needing it anymore."[19]
"No one cares about/loves me."
"I'm a failure. I'll never be what I thought I could be."

From these statements you can see that some verbal clues would seem to indicate suicidal intention only if other clues were present, whereas other statements are fairly clear signals of intent.

An example may help emphasize the importance of picking up on a harmless-sounding statement when it is in fact one of a cluster of clues. A woman called late one night to check on a friend, Sally, who had been depressed lately and was recovering from being rejected by a boyfriend who had recently married someone else. After a brief visit on the phone, Sally said, "I'm just so sleepy, I can't even talk." After a couple of other similar protests, the friend replied, "Okay, I'll call you later." What the friend did not know was that Sally had taken a lethal dose of barbiturates. Sally died before midnight.

With Sally there was a cluster of clues. She had previously attempted suicide twice. She had a history of depression. Recently she had suffered the loss of a relationship through rejection. With these clues, the verbal statements about such heavy sleepiness became very significant.

Obviously the friend felt guilty for not checking out what was going on with Sally, and it is easy for us with the history before us to feel we would have handled it differently. In any event, Sally illustrates once more the importance of seeing the clues, understanding their meaning, and checking further to see if they do in fact signal suicidal intention.

In reality, Sally illustrates something else. Her final suicide attempt was very well planned. She knew just how much medicine to take and how long it would require to take effect. She gave out few signals of her intentions and even called several friends that night without leaving with any of them the hint of suicide. Sally once again illustrates that once a person has firmly resolved to take his life, he is very difficult to stop. Fortunately, most suicidal persons do not have such firm resolve.

Conclusion

In going back over this chapter, I realize that so many clues to suicidal behavior have been mentioned that you may feel a bit overwhelmed or you may feel that I have done nothing more than increase your paranoia about suicide. I hope I have neither overwhelmed you nor created paranoia. The clues to suicide are so diverse that to simplify them any further than I already have would be to oversimplify. Therefore, I have chosen to present the diversity and trust you to use the "spirit of discernment."

Having looked at all these signs to suicide, though, may have raised within you the question, "Now that I know the signs, what do I do about them?" That is what the next chapter is about.

4

How Can I Help?

THE THOUGHT OF HAVING someone close to you commit suicide may be so frightening that you are paralyzed by that fright. In the face of a possible suicide, you may be so repulsed by the thought that you run from reality. But as the mother of a young man who took his life told me, "Tell parents that it can happen to their children. No family is immune."

If suicide can happen to those around us and to those we love, can we help prevent it? Yes. Your ability to help implies responsibility, and we cannot escape that responsibility by claiming there is nothing we can do. We must say also that there are certainly limits to our ability to help and limits to our responsibility.

In this chapter, we will consider ways to assess the risk of suicide, specific strategies of intervention, means of getting the person professional help, and the need to continue to be a supporter/friend to the suicidal person. What I have not included here are the broader issues of how you can help a suicidal person in your family or among your friends. Issues such as communication, conflict resolution, self-esteem, and trust could be included as ways to prevent suicide. These should not be neglected, but I will trust you to seek out good books on parenting, marriage, and friendship as your sources for help on the broader aspects of relationships. For our purposes here, I have focused more directly on helping the person who is actually or potentially suicidal.

Assessing the Risk

Although the previous chapter on signs of suicide dealt some with the risk factor, our attention focuses here on specific ways to assess the immediate risk of suicide. In order to do such assessment, you have to take some risks. Those risks include having the person become angry with you, accuse you of prying, withdraw from you, or seek to make you an accomplice in what he does. When broaching the subject of suicide with another person, you have to realize there are some risks, but I maintain that the risks are worth taking. For we are, after all, talking about trying to prevent someone's death. Also, I should add that I have never had a hostile response.

Having noted that the suicidal person is angry and that anger is often turned in upon himself, do not run if the person begins to get angry with you. That anger directed at you may be a healthy step as the person begins to defuse the anger he has for himself. You do not want to provoke him, but being able to absorb some of the anger without becoming defensive or retaliatory can be a powerful statement of the degree of concern you have.

One risk which should not hinder you is the notion that if you mention suicide, it will only give the person the idea. Either the person has thought about it and will probably welcome the chance to talk with someone about those thoughts, or he has not thought about it and your mentioning it will almost certainly not lead him in that direction. As noted earlier, with some persons you may want to avoid using the word "suicide" when inquiring about this possibility.

1. Raise the question

The basic rule of thumb is, "When in doubt, check it out." Begin by mentioning some of the things you have noticed that have made you concerned about the person. Here you do not need even to hint at the possibility of suicide. After mentioning the things that have concerned you, ask something like, "Can you help me understand what is going on?" After you have listened carefully, then if the person's response warrants it, you may ask, "Have you come to the place that you have been thinking of harming yourself/taking your life/committing suicide?" This question obviously needs to be asked in private and in a caring, nonjudgmental way.

Some suggest not mentioning the word *suicide;* others say you should. I think that will be a judgment call depending on your relationship with the person, your perception of him, and the "feel" of the moment.

Do not be put off by a joking or mildly hostile reply. Pursue it further by saying something like, "No, I'm serious. You seem so down and frustrated that I thought you might have been thinking about it. Honestly, are you?"

With this kind of openness, most people who have been contemplating suicide will respond genuinely. If they do not, your option is to drop the matter for the moment and either raise it at another time or talk with other persons close to the individual about what you fear.

If the person seems despondent, yet does not indicate he has been thinking about suicide, you can make a mini-contract with him by saying, "Well, if you get to that point, will you promise me you will talk with me about it?" Get some kind of affirmative response to this question. Eye contact here is important because that helps to seal the promise.

2. Discover the intended method

If the person indicates he has been thinking about suicide, you need to find out how he would do it. Simply ask, "Have you thought about how you would harm yourself/take your life?"

If the response is, "No, I haven't thought about that," then the immediate risk is probably not as great. You still need to explore with this person what suicide means for him, help him to put into focus the problems he is facing, and then see what further help may be needed. More will be said about getting further help in a later section of this chapter.

The person who has thought about how he would take his life is one step closer to death by suicide. *The more specific his plan is, the greater the risk of suicide.*

If the suicide plan is bizarre, realize that the person may be exhibiting some form of mental illness. If this is the case, this person needs medical attention as soon as possible.

3. Assess the lethality of the method

How deadly is the method this person has chosen? How certain is death if this method is used? These are extremely important questions for you to determine.

If the method is very lethal, such as using a gun or hanging himself, the danger is greater than if the person is planning to slash his wrists or take pills. These latter methods certainly can be lethal and should be taken seriously, but there is often less risk with these methods than some others.

Another factor to consider is whether the person has accurate knowledge about the effectiveness of the method he has chosen. An adolescent may think that taking a whole bottle of aspirin will kill him. (Under certain conditions, it could.) The person's perception of the deadliness of the chosen method is important to know. If he *thinks* the method is lethal, then he is serious about taking his life.

4. Determine the availability of the method

How available is the method chosen? If the person plans to use a gun, does he have one? If so, are bullets available? Is the gun loaded? Where is the gun?

If the method is readily available or if there is a specific plan to obtain the method, the risk is increased.

Obviously if the person is carrying around with him his instrument of destruction, he is serious and may be close to suicide.

5. Judge the amount of disturbance

Edwin Shneidman lists "perturbation" as one of the determining factors in assessing the risk of suicide. By this he means the degree of psychic upheaval and disorganization. Though this level of disturbance is not in itself a certain sign of high risk, combined with an intended method of high lethality it certainly is. Also, a person may show few signs of disturbance and still take his life.[1]

6. Explore personal history

Knowing whether or not previous attempts have been made, if there has been a suicide in the family, the person has a history of mental illness, or there have been recent upheavals and losses, will all aid in the assessment of risk. It is important that these questions be asked carefully, not as if you are running through a checklist or giving the person the "third degree."

When assessing risk, even when you have determined the risk is not high, there is still cause for concern, and a specific plan of seeking help for the person should be developed and discussed. More will be said about this later. It should be noted also that suicide sometimes occurs even when the risk was not determined to be high. We can be careful in this area and still be fooled. Especially when the suicidal person is an alcoholic, impulsive, or psychotic, the degree of unpredictability is increased.

Where an attempt has occurred or is discovered before the attempt was actually made, Aaron Beck and his colleagues have identified the main characteristics that suggest serious suicidal intent. These characteristics are as follows:

1. Carried out in isolation;
2. Times so that intervention is unlikely;
3. Precautions taken to avoid discovery;
4. Preparations made in anticipation of death;
5. Other people informed beforehand of the individual's intention;
6. Extensive premeditation;
7. Suicide note left;
8. Failure to alert other people following the attempt.[2]

The authors of the article reporting Beck's findings also make this concluding remark, "The patient who after an attempt is upset at his or her failure should always be hospitalized."[3]

Specific Strategies of Intervention

Knowing that a person is potentially suicidal, what do you do? Because we are talking about such issues as risk assessment and strategies of intervention, this should not imply that you must seek by yourself to prevent a suicide or that you should take on the job of counseling a suicidal person. In some extreme emergencies, you may have to work alone, but that is not the ideal. I am assuming that you may find yourself in a situation where you are confronted with a person who is suicidal and you want to know how to handle such a situation. This information is for you and you will find it helpful. But realize that after determining the risk and further talking with the person, you should seek help beyond your own resources for a suicidal person. I am attempting to help you become an informed helper, not a Lone Ranger assigned to suicide prevention. This caution needs to be mentioned lest, in your desire to help, you run the risk of "getting in over your head." There is a fine line between overestimating your power in these situations and underestimating that power.

1. Use the power of interest and concern

In walking the fine line between feeling too much power and feeling powerless, realize that the primary power you have in dealing with a suicidal person is your relationship with him and the way you show interest and concern. In the midst of a suicidal crisis, that gives you power if the interest and concern are genuine. Wisely use that power to avert the potential suicide.

This raises the question, though, "Am I the right person to be trying to talk him/her out of suicide?" If you are the only person available, then you are the right person. But if other family members or other significant persons in whom the suicidal person trusts and to whom he responds are near or can be reached by phone, then it may be wise to call them in for aid. This should be done particularly if your relationship to the person is hostile or has been strained. If that hostility or strain continues to be exhibited, then you may not be the right person for the moment. In fact, the suicidal individual could even set you up to be the "cause" of his eventual suicide if he is hostile enough. Also, you may not be the right person for this situation if past experiences have substantially eroded the potential of a relationship. Unless in this moment that relationship can be resurrected, your power may not be substantial in the midst of this crisis.

However, do not use the question, "Am I the right person?" as an escape from responsibility. You may feel, "Surely someone else can handle this better than I," but the reality may be that at the moment you are the best person.

In the midst of this conversation continually be looking for significant people in the life of the suicidal person who may be important in stopping this suicide. This person may or may not be a family member, but it will be someone who is a positive and supportive influence on the life of the suicidal one. After checking out further the nature of the relationship with this person or persons, ask the suicidal one's permission to involve these significant others in this effort to prevent the suicide. This can be one of the most important steps in the intervention.

When we talk about the power of interest and concern, the reality must be faced that some depressed and/or suicidal persons will abuse that interest and concern. Many psychiatrists refuse to see a person they deem to be a "manipulative depressive." That refusal is because of the time these persons require, the demands they make, and their seeming lack of desire to change. This kind of person is usually truly depressed, but he uses that depression to get attention, time, and other things he desires. When is this person merely being manipulative, and when is he seriously suicidal? Unfortunately even many professionals cannot always make that distinction. But the rule of thumb throughout this book has been to take any suicide threat seriously. Does that set you up to become vulnerable to the manipulative person who learns that he can "ring your bell" by a threat of suicide? In one sense, yes, because to love another is to make yourself vulnerable. Therefore, with the manipulator we at times open ourselves to being used as the price we pay for caring.

The other side of the coin is that when we are being used by someone, we feel anger toward him and especially so as he plays on our desire to help. Without some guidelines in such a relationship, the anger builds toward rejection and then little help can be provided.

Consider then some guidelines for dealing with manipulative persons.

First, set reasonable limits. When this person calls just to talk, early in the conversation let him know how much time you have. For instance, "Yes, I've got ten minutes to visit." Be firm and straightforward about what you will and will not do. If you just cannot talk at this time, set up an exact time when you will return his call. Second, help the person to deal with the consequences of his actions. Do not be his rescuer from every difficult situation he gets himself into. Rather than being the rescuer, help him explore problem-solving options. Third, have someone you can "blow off some steam" with about this relationship. Fourth, gain some perspective on what you are getting from this relationship. Though you may feel put upon and used and angry, you may have gotten into this difficult place because you virtually invited the other person to use you so you could feel needed. Fifth, when appropriate, share with the manipulative person some of your feelings of anger at being manipulated.

All this must be done carefully and appropriately and not in such a way that you seem to be saying the person really has not been hurting. When sharing these feelings, guard against being provoked by him into an outburst of anger that he can then use as his "reason" for a suicide attempt. One of the best times to share such feelings is just prior to a time the person will be with another friend or his therapist. This gives him a third party to talk with about your confrontation.

Sixth, I have assumed in what I have said here that this person has sought professional help or is in therapy. If he is not, he most likely should be. Especially if you are a family member, it could be helpful for both of you to have some sessions together with the therapist.

Having now taken these two diversions from the primary point of this subsection, let me briefly stress that point again: by the very act of showing interest and concern, you gain some power to prevent suicide.

2. Pray

Claim God's promise of power through prayer. Ask God to intervene in this circumstance. Pray for yourself that you may be guided by God's Spirit to say and do what is best. Pray for the other person that he may glimpse again the dream of hope within him rather than his nightmare of despair. Realize that your concern can be to the person an incarnation of the love of God. God can speak through your actions.

You may choose to have verbal prayer with the person, including asking him also to pray. Be aware that, on the one hand, we can use prayer rather glibly. On the other hand, with some people we are too hesitant to pray in their presence or to invite them to join us in prayer.

When praying aloud with a distraught person, avoid trying to make him feel guilty or foolish for what he is feeling or considering. Avoid being morbid. Be hopeful and genuine. Avoid communicating impatience, anger, or leaving the impression that prayer is a way to get rid of the person.

A suicidal crisis can be an opportunity to give a word of witness to the abundant life available through Jesus Christ without implying there is something wrong with the suicidal person because he is not presently experiencing the abundance. This word of witness should be not only verbal but also active as "the word becomes flesh."

I recently heard again the testimony of a friend, a doctor who also became a drug addict. Bob knew he might eventually take his life by drugs, but he persisted in his bondage to narcotics. After he had spent a night at the hospital alternating between semiconsciousness and enough consciousness to inject more sodium pentothal into his veins, a fellow doctor found him passed out the next morning in the doctors' lounge. The doctor who found him was a dedicated Christian. He witnessed to Bob, took him into his home, got him in touch with organizations that work with alcohol and drug abusers, and invited him to church. Though Bob had earlier rejected the Christian faith, he soon became a Christian, is now active in the church, and shares his testimony with many others. God intervened through another person to prevent what surely would have been a suicide. Bob's Christian friend became Christ to him in that moment of need. The friend exhibited prayer in its truest form—the prayer was part and parcel of wise ministry. You can read of Bob's experience in his book, *Prescription for Addiction* (Robert Gehring, Zondervan, 1984).

3. Build the relationship

Seek to build the relationship with the person by listening carefully, patiently, and openly. Try not to show shock or disdain. Exhibit all the feelings of competence you can muster. Do not get into a hand-wringing nervousness that communicates, "This scares me to death, and I don't know what to do!"

Avoid denial. Faced with a person who mentions suicide, you may be tempted to say, "Oh, you really don't mean it," or "You wouldn't do that." He may even say he agrees with you, though internally he is still mulling the possibility in his mind.

One form of denial to avoid is rejecting as silly or ridiculous the reasons a person mentions for considering suicide. If these reasons have driven him to the brink of suicide, they are very real to him. In his book on suicide, Alvarez notes, "As in love, things which seem trivial to the outsider, tiresome or amusing, assume enormous importance to those in the grip of the monster, while the sanest arguments against it seem to them simply absurd."[4]

Listen reflectively. Seek to be a sounding board for the distressed person's feelings and thoughts. You may say something like this, "If I understand you right, you're feeling there's no way out of this and there's no one who can really help you?" Whatever you say, you are seeking to reflect to the person some of what you hear him saying. This allows him to know he is being heard, gives you a reading on the accuracy of your listening, and helps the other person begin to focus his thoughts and feelings.

Be hopeful without being unduly optimistic. You want to reflect hope but not deny the reality of the situation. Especially avoid false reassurance. "Oh, I just know it will all work out" is cold comfort if the person sees no way any of it will "work out."

In this stage of building the relationship, you are basically seeking to listen, understand, and reflect. Do not challenge or confront at this point, and do not begin too quickly to start "doing something" before you have listened carefully.

One element of caring that should not be ignored is touch. To a frightened suicidal person, the touch of a friend's hand, an arm around the shoulder, or a hug, can be powerful. When one feels he is slipping away from life, the touch of a caring person can be a gentle but potent reminder of his contact with the living.

If you are talking to the person on the telephone, keep him talking. If you do not know exactly where the person is, try to find out. If the risk of suicide seems high and you are with someone else, urge that person to try to get a family member or friend to go to where he is. In some areas, the telephone company will cooperate by tracing the call if the person refuses to disclose his location.

4. Help focus the problems and resources

The suicidal individual is usually in a state of confusion. Either he is confused about his feelings and why he feels them, or he may be very clear about his feelings and still remain confused about his alternatives. Also, most suicidal persons fail to see the resources available to help them cope.

Not in an argumentative way, but in a vein of gentle exploring, help the person begin to identify clearly the nature of the problems he faces and his alternatives. Do not be put off by his "Yes, but—" responses to your suggestions. He probably feels he has considered every option. With some persistence, though, you may be able to spark a flame of hope. In any event, seek to bring some order out of the confusion you observe.

What resources are available to this person? What about family, friends, faith, activities? If you do not know him well, find out something about family and friends. Who is he close to? Who does he speak most warmly about? Be careful that you do not assume too much about family relationships. You may attempt to motivate a person by appealing to his concern about how much his suicide would hurt, for instance, his mother. That may be, in part, what he wants to do. On the other hand, where there are particularly warm relationships, those may be the best "bargaining chips" you have.

In mentioning the resource of faith, here, too, wrong assumptions can be made about what will deter a person from suicide. For example, conjuring up an image of how the person will burn in hell could feed directly into his desire to be punished if he is feeling particularly guilty. In contrast, some images you could paint about the beauty of heaven might draw him closer to suicide. In any event, in this as in other areas, you need to listen carefully so that you understand the person's perception of something you might consider a suicide deterrent. Do not assume it would deter him until you have raised the issue and have seen how he responds.

5. Confront romantic notions of death

Especially with adolescents, romantic notions of death abound and lurk behind their images of suicide. They fantasize themselves beautifully laid out like Snow White while everyone comes by and exclaims how great they were. They see the attention the death of a fellow teenager elicits and imagine themselves dead and the center of all that attention. Also, because death seems so far away and they seem so invulnerable to the ravages of illness and age, teenagers often envision death as only a quiet, dreamy sleep.

These erroneous notions of death and its aftermath should be confronted. Death is not friend. As the apostle Paul states, death is the enemy. Confronted with the cold, hard realities of death and the short attention span of grieving friends, many teenagers may reassess the "beauty" of suicide. Remind the person that while there is life, changes can be made, but death is irreversible. Someone has commented, "Suicide is a permanent solution to a temporary problem."

6. Deal with the method

Most suicidal persons have an attachment to the method they have chosen to use in killing themselves. Somehow the method symbolizes something for them, and they do not want to be deterred from using that means of suicide. Alvarez contends, "People try to die more by the means than by the end, just as a sexual fetishist gets more satisfaction from his rituals than from the orgasm to which they lead."[5]

If you can keep the suicidal individual from using or getting his chosen method, that one step may prevent his suicide. If the person has an attachment to a certain gun, a particular kind of medication, or a specific knife, either ask him to give that to you, or in his absence remove it. In one case, a father who was alert to his son's depression hid the shells to the son's favorite shotgun. That action of his father, the son later told me, prevented his suicide.

In another case, a sixteen-year-old boy who was fascinated with guns talked his mother into allowing him to keep just one gun out of his collection though he was in counseling for depression and suicidal thoughts. The week before Christmas, with the sole gun left from his collection, he took his life.

If the suicidal person is armed with a knife, gun, or other weapon, do not try to take it from him forcibly. This show of force may only trigger his suicidal urge, force him to turn on you, or result in a serious accident. Seek patiently and gently to talk him out of attempting the suicide and ask him to surrender the weapon to you. Be cautious about a person who smiles slyly when giving up his means for suicide. The smile may be saying, "You think you've won this battle, but I have other means." Check to see if he is harboring a back-up method such as another gun or another bottle of pills. If drugs have been taken, you need to know what and how many and how long ago. Has he also been drinking alcohol? All this information needs to be relayed to the emergency medical team who will take the person to the hospital unless you take the person yourself. If the person is calling by phone, have him open his door so that the persons coming to take him to the hospital can get in. If you transport the person, be sure to take the pill container and any leftover pills.

The same kind of specific information needs to be obtained when other methods of suicide are involved. If the person has slashed his wrists, how long ago and how much bleeding is there? If he has called you and he is threatening a jump, where exactly is he, what is his plan, and has he been drinking? If he has a gun, has he been drinking and are others in danger? Drinking alcohol heightens the risk in each of these instances. If you know a suicide is in progress with a gun and you call police, be sure to inform them that the person is armed.[6]

In each of these instances, you can see the need to avoid panic so you can get the needed information and act deliberately. This controlled response also helps the suicidal person have confidence you are decisively helping him. Do not act so coolly, though, that you fail to communicate warmth and concern.

7. Spread out the responsibility

When someone tells you he has considered suicide, that puts a heavy weight on your shoulders. You now know this person's "secret"—a secret so powerful it may end in death. Can you bear the burden of that secret alone?

To be the only person to know of these suicidal intentions is too much for you to bear alone. Do not promise to keep this information only to yourself. Negotiate as to whom you will talk to about this. If the person asked for a promise of confidentiality prior to revealing his suicide aims, and you granted his request, you must now explain that it would be irresponsible for you to keep it to yourself.

Certainly if the individual persists in his resolve to take his life, stay with him and continue talking, but also try to contact his family physician, a close relative, a counselor whom he has previously seen, or, if he has not seen one, a counselor who is adept at handling this kind of situation. To have someone who knows the person is best, but if this is not possible, contact a suicide prevention center, mental health center, the emergency unit of a hospital, or the police, if they have someone trained to deal with this kind of emergency.

If the person has significantly changed in his perception of his problems and he is no longer talking about taking his life, some agreement should still be reached about what counseling he will seek and when. I will deal with this in more detail later in the chapter. This should also be followed up by your talking with the family members and/or friends you have both agreed upon. You can also involve friends and family in a support system without revealing the suicide threat. You may say something like, "Sue has been down lately. Will you try to stay in touch with her or just include her in some things you are doing?" Do not, however, overdo this lest the person feel his privacy has been invaded.

8. Make a contract with the person

Even when a person has stopped talking about taking his life, how do you know he really will not? Of course, there is no absolute guarantee, but a verbal contract can be one more preventive measure that decreases the possibility of suicide.

Many a friend—and many a counselor—can report talking to someone who was very depressed and even suicidal, who, after the talk, exclaimed how much better he felt, only to have that person then leave and later commit suicide. Do not accept on face value such statements as, "Thanks, I feel so much better now." It is still not time to begin patting yourself on the back.

Consider making a verbal contract. This device is most crucial if there is a time lag before the person is able to see a counselor or psychiatrist or other professional. You ask the person to agree that he will get in touch with you or some other agreed-upon person if he gets suicidal. The agreement is stated in this way: "I will contact you or _____ if I begin thinking about taking my life. Even if I have trouble reaching you, I will keep on until I have talked to one of you about these thoughts of suicide."

Notice that the word *try* is not used since anyone can say, "But I tried to reach you." Note also the firm resolve of the word *will* and the second sentence which also closes off the option of having "tried" to get in contact. Obviously in such circumstances, you will want to stay where the person can reach you, but there simply may be times, however brief, when you cannot be contacted. Also, you would surely alert the back-up person referred to in the contract about this agreement.

In making this verbal contract, ask the person if he will agree to it. If he will, then ask him to repeat it word for word out loud. If there is hesitation in his voice, ask him to repeat it again with conviction. If he again fails to sound as if he means it, tell him you sense he is insincere. Ask him to tell you what keeps him from wanting to make that contract. After having talked about it, then come back and ask him to make the contract.

If the person later gets into counseling, this contract may have to be renegotiated so the the counselor becomes the primary helper and the suicidal person does not continue to use you as his counselor. You will still provide support and help, but at that point his counseling needs to be done by the counselor.

9. Develop a plan of action

A person who is down enough to contemplate suicide needs some specific steps to take that will give him a sense of accomplishment in making some progress against the problems he faces. He also needs to alter some behaviors that are contributing to the problems.

If the individual has moved beyond his resolve or wish for suicide, begin to formulate with him some specific steps to deal with his problems and to help him feel better. These steps are *in addition to* and not instead of getting professional help.

You may start this development of a plan of action by saying something like, "As I see it, you have three basic problems that are giving you trouble." List those problems and ask if you have been accurate. When you have agreed on the problems, ask, "On this first one, what can you do to deal with that?" Attempt to keep him involved in seeking solutions rather than to provide all the answers for him. If he honestly seems not to be able to generate any alternatives, then aid him. But be wary of the person's lack of involvement in this process or his lack of enthusiasm. Both may be signs of how deep the depression is or how unresolved the suicidal thoughts are.

In developing the plan of action, do not make it so sweeping or so difficult that the plan itself seems overwhelming. Consider steps such as making some changes in routine or environment, engaging in some form of recreation or taking a trip, getting in touch with an old friend, starting a new hobby or reviving an old one. Simply the addition of regular exercise can be a powerful deterrent as some of the energy given to suicidal thoughts is displaced and the brain's natural antidepressants become activated by vigorous exercise. Larger changes may also be examined such as changing schools or jobs, getting vocational guidance, consulting a financial counselor or a credit counselor, changing a major in school, altering a relationship, or shifting some responsibilities. As ideas such as these are generated, the enthusiasm can build as the person begins to see that the problems really can be handled if broken down into smaller pieces.

This sounds easy and simple, and I know it is rarely that way, but it is very important. The development of a plan of action will help the person have some sense of power over his problems and provide him with specific steps to carry out. This gives him a measure of hope and therefore an orientation to the future.

10. A few don'ts

Do not try to shock or challenge the person. Do not, for instance, dare him to go ahead and take his life. This kind of daring is dangerous and is not a deterrent.

Do not try to mind-read or psychoanalyze. Do not impose your interpretation on the situation or try to tell the person what he is "really feeling or thinking." Do not try to take on the job of analyzing psychological motivations.

Do not belittle or try to shame the person. This kind of approach can only make matters worse.

Do not try to argue or get into a philosophical discussion. An argument is not going to settle or help anything in a suicidal crisis. Philosophical debates need to be held at another time, not when a person is suicidal.

Getting the Person Professional Help

If a person has become suicidal, you can assume he needs professional help. Even when the risk of suicide seems low or the person seems better, getting the person to a competent professional is important. Do not rely too heavily on your own assessment or ability to handle the situation.

When broaching the subject of referral to a professional, mention this possibility in a way that will not give the suicidal person the idea that you are rejecting him. Let him know that you will continue to stay in touch with him, and that his getting professional help will in no way end your helping him. Deal carefully and firmly with a response such as, "I came to you for help and now you're sending me off to someone else. I thought you would help me." Assure the person that one of the best ways you can help him is by seeing that he gets the kind of care he needs.

When you mention the possibility of his seeing a psychiatrist or some other professional, the person may become alarmed since he may take this as a signal that you think he is crazy. Again, reassurance is needed here. Explain that seeing a professional does not imply that he is crazy. Many people we come in contact with every day are seeing psychiatrists, psychologists, and other persons in the helping professions. Most of these people are functioning quite well but have come to a time in their lives when they need some help.

If the suicidal person is a Christian, he may feel that to go to a professional counselor is an evidence of a lack of faith. A medical analogy is often helpful here. If a person has a physical problem that needs attention, seeking a doctor's help is not a lack of faith. Prayer and faith continue to be a part of the process as you pray for God's help, and you do so with the faith that the help of God is present. God uses the doctor as an instrument of healing. Even so, when a psychological problem arises, prayer and faith are utilized and the counselor becomes a part of the healing. The counselor becomes one of God's ministers of healing.

If the referral is still resisted, be firm and direct, explaining that you feel the risk is sufficient to warrant further help. Do not attempt scare tactics, but help the person face the gravity of the situation. Try to discover what fears prevent him from seeking more help. Does he fear hospitalization? Is the expense a factor? Have there been other persons this individual has known who have had bad experiences with counselors? Try to answer these objections carefully and with the best information you have. Continue the reassurances that you will not abandon him.

This process of convincing the person to seek professional help may take time, but patiently persevere. As has been mentioned before, many an individual has gotten his problems "off his chest" in talking to a friend only later to return to his suicidal notions. If the person simply refuses to see a professional, tell him that you cannot keep this information about his suicide thoughts to yourself. Let him know you feel compelled for his sake and yours to contact someone who can be of help.

Who do you contact, though, for that help? If the person is acutely suicidal, has already made an attempt, shows signs of considerable disturbance and agitation, or if he has lost touch with reality, then medical help is needed immediately. A family physician may be contacted as the first line of defense. If you know the psychiatrist or if the person has seen a psychiatrist, get in touch with him. An admission to a hospital may be required, and you will need a medical doctor for this.

Be on guard, though, for either a general physician or a psychiatrist who only sees the patient, prescribes some medication, and tells the patient to go home and rest. The suicidal person needs more help than that. The doctor should be willing to talk to the person for at least an hour, and if he does not admit the patient to a hospital, he should agree to see the person again soon. If you feel the doctor is not taking the situation seriously enough, talk to him about your concern. If you are still not satisfied, seek other medical help. Remember that even well-trained doctors make mistakes, too.

If the person is not acutely suicidal, you may consider a nonmedical professional. If the person has already seen a counselor, contact that person. Explain the situation as you understand it and find out when the suicidal person can be seen by the counselor. If the appointment date is too far off, appeal to the counselor to set up an earlier time or ask him to refer you to someone else.

What if there is no one in the helping professions who has seen this person? From all the help available, how do you choose the best counselor/therapist? If you know of other persons who have had contact with such professionals, contact them. Your minister can be a significant help here, as can persons who themselves have been in counseling.

Should you only refer to a Christian counselor? That is a difficult question. If there are trained, experienced Christian counselors available, then by all means seek their help. Realize, though, that not every person who hangs out a shingle as a Christian counselor has the training and experience necessary to work with a suicidal person. Does this Christian counselor have graduate training in psychology? Is he certified by responsible professional groups? Does he make referrals to psychiatrists when the case warrants it? Does he work alone or in consultation with other professionals? In other words, do not refer to a Christian counselor simply because he uses the title "Christian counselor." Make sure he is a trained, experienced, responsible counselor.

Other sources of referral include psychologists, pastoral counselors, clinical social workers, marriage and family therapists, and hospital chaplains. The following explanation concerning the training and professional credentials of all the possible sources of referral should enable you to make the best choice in getting the help you need. It is quite legitimate to inquire about or ask to see the credentials of the person you are thinking of consulting.

— *Psychiatrists* are medical doctors who have special training in psychiatry. They are able to prescribe drugs and admit persons to hospitals. A reputable psychiatrist should have a valid state license and certification by the American Board of Psychiatry and Neurology or board eligibility.

—*Clinical psychologists* generally have a doctoral degree in psychology plus at least a year of supervised clinical training. A clinical psychologist should have a state license (where required) and certification by the American Board of Examiners in Professional Psychology or clinical membership in other professional groups.

—*Pastoral counselors* are ministers who have special training in counseling. They may hold membership in the American Association of Pastoral Counselors.

—*Clinical social workers* have a master's and sometimes a doctor's degree in mental health. Accreditation by the Academy of Certified Social Workers is usual.

—*Marriage and family therapists* have graduate training in psychology and have had supervision in counseling couples and families though they also see individuals. Ask about clinical membership in the American Association for Marriage and Family Therapy.

—*Hospital chaplains* often have training in counseling, though some do not. Most have membership in such organizations as the American College of Chaplains, the American Association of Clinical Pastoral Education, the American Association of Pastoral Counselors, or the American Association for Marriage and Family Therapy.

Other sources of referral include the local mental health center, a suicide prevention center, a nearby medical school, a family service agency, or a child guidance clinic.

Having made the referral, check to see if the person follows up by keeping the appointment and remaining in counseling. If he does not, you can encourage him to do so, but ultimately you cannot force him to get help. The exception to that occurs when the person is acutely suicidal and/or psychotic, and you seek some kind of commitment to a hospital. If you are dealing with a person who is this far in his journey toward suicide, you need to learn the laws of your state about temporary commitment. Also, if the suicide attempt is about to happen or if the suicidal person is endangering the life of others and will not seek other help, the police may need to be called. Your hope here is that your local police have been trained to handle suicidal crises.

If the person has followed up by getting into counseling, how do you know if that counseling is helping? First, do not expect a "quick fix." The suicide process has taken a long time to develop and will take time to be reversed. If it is possible, talk to the counselor and get his perspective on the situation and the progress that is being made. After some period of time, if you do not feel good progress is being made, talk with the counselor and share your feelings with him. If you still come away dissatisfied, then raise the issue with your family member or friend who is in counseling and consider together the option of seeking other help. This should be done with caution, though, because it is difficult to build up the trust level necessary for a good counseling relationship. Also, if the counselee is getting angry with the counselor, you might interpret this as negative whereas it may be positive. The person may be beginning to direct outward some of the anger that had been turned inward.

Basically, you want to find a counselor who is warm, empathetic, nonjudgmental, genuine, and able to inspire hope and trust. Important also, if the person is seeing a nonmedical counselor, is the counselor's willingness and ability to make referrals or have consultations with a psychiatrist in case medication or hospitalization is needed. In the case of teenagers, a counselor should be sought who related well to teenagers. My personal bias is that the counselor should be eclectic in his approach, that is, not tied exclusively to one method or school of psychotherapy. Generally, in the case of suicide, I would shy away from a counselor who seemed intent only on helping the counselee have better insight into why he feels what he does. Studies indicate that with suicidal persons a more active, somewhat more directive approach including behavior modification techniques is more helpful.

Finally, a part of the referral process should be a thorough physical by a medical doctor. Hypothyroidism (low thyroid function), diabetes, or viral pneumonia, for instance, could be contributing to the depression. Also, some drugs such as sleep aids, antihypertension drugs, and even some contraceptives can produce or exacerbate depression.

What Schools Can Do

Because I have been asked to speak to groups of school personnel and have done continuing education workshops for them, I have often dealt with the question of what schools can do in suicide prevention.

First, with the students, work indirectly on the issue. The atmosphere of the school is crucial. If the school conveys directly and in many subtle ways that this is a positive place where people care about students—and a place that helps students realize their dreams for the future—you have done a lot right there toward suicide deterrence. On another "suicidal" issue, that of teenage pregnancy, I recently heard a radio interview with a woman who had just completed and published a major study of teenage pregnancy. She said, "The best contraceptive is a sense of the future." If all of the students in a high school, from the honors English student to the future auto mechanic in vocational education, has a sense of the future, the threat of suicide is lessened.

Another indirect way of working with the students is to provide positive niches for them. I realize that extracurricular activities can be overdone in schools, but adolescents are going to group themselves in some fashion. What I am recommending is that involvement in groups like math club, band, choir, athletics, pep squad, rodeo club, and other groups be encouraged as a way to help the students find a positive place. The isolated adolescent is in danger from many things, and one of them is suicide.

You will notice that I have indicated indirect methods of suicide prevention with the youth. I believe that indirect methods should be employed in a school or school system unless something has occurred that has caused suicide to be the focus of many of the students' attention. If that situation arises because of the suicide of one of their peers or a series of suicides by students, then I think school-wide assemblies, special speakers in classes, and the availability of special counseling for dealing with suicidal thoughts is appropriate. But I am convinced that in an environment where suicide is not obviously on the minds of many students, harm can be done by doing "a big splash" about suicide. Yes, I do think too much attention in the name of prevention can create a dangerous atmosphere in which suicide, however unintentionally, becomes suggested as an option.

I do believe, however, that school personnel should deal with the issue directly as individual students display suicidal thoughts and behavior. That is the purpose of the much-needed training of school personnel on initial intervention.

On this issue of direct/indirect dealing with the issue of suicide, I draw from a study done of approximately 1,000 students ranging in age from 13 to 18. They were exposed to one of three different suicide education programs in six different schools. Concerning this, a group of writers concludes:

> The findings thus do little to support the value of general educational programs. Most students do not need them, and those who do would probably be better served by an individualized approach to their clinical problems. This is not to say, however, that there is no place in the high school curriculum for more education about mental health and how to obtain help for emotional disorder.[7]

Second, inform all school personnel about the danger signs of suicide, what to do in response, and where to get more help for the student. By all school personnel, I mean *all school personnel.* Train not only the teachers and the administrative staff, but also train the bus drivers, cafeteria workers, aides, and custodians. Much of this training is available on film and/or videotape. Sometimes it is best done "in house" with local school personnel, but sometimes you are better served to bring in an outside professional to do the training. The American Association of Suicidology (2459 South Ash, Denver, Colorado 80222) can provide guidance toward materials and speakers.

Third, inform the parents. Through such organizations as the P.T.A. and other special programs, parents can be informed about warning signs and responses to make when the warning signs point in a dangerous direction. Recognize as you make this effort to inform parents that some of the very parents you want to attend will not. On the other hand, some of the healthiest, most well-adjusted kids' parents will be there. That is just the way it is going to be. It is worth the effort, nevertheless, and even that healthy kid may someday be at a dangerous point where an intervention is needed. In regard to those parents who do not come as you wished they would, you may want to follow up the meeting for parents with articles in the newspaper using information supplied to the newspaper by you.

Fourth, provide specific help for students at risk. As students at risk are identified by various school personnel, special programs, counseling, and support groups need to be set up. The basic purpose of these is to guide the student to re-decide for life and to close that escape hatch of suicide. In other words, the student who has vowed, "If it ever gets bad enough, I can always take my life," or "I'll show them; I'll kill myself," needs to be led to the place where he sees the futility of that option of suicide. Obviously with many of these students the complicating factors such as drug abuse, family dysfunction, and emotional disturbance will also have to be dealt with. In most cases, though not all, the situation will be improved if the student's family can be involved in the help.

Finally, provide follow-up for students in trouble. When students fail, or perceive that they have failed—academically, athletically, or socially—they are at higher risk of suicide. The tricky thing about this, of course, is that students respond in such varied ways to "failure." Many seem nonchalant, while others quickly resolve to do better. But some start telling themselves things like "I am a failure. I never will be any good." "If I can't do this, then I don't want to live." Therefore, although it is difficult to maintain this kind of special attention, school personnel need to be trained to watch out for the student who has failed, "messed-up," or perceives that he has.

A tragic example of the need for this kind of follow-up is found in this note by a high school senior who killed himself in Fort Worth, Texas, in the winter of 1988. The following is one of the five notes he left behind:

Dear Dad,

I'm sorry I had to do this but it was the only way out for me. I got kicked out of school yesterday. I couldn't face you because I was so ashamed. Tell Jerry, Mom, Chuck, and the rest of my friends & relatives I'm going to miss them and I love them.

'Bye
Love you
Mike

P.S.
Make sure
these letters
get to the people
I addressed them to.

Here is the money to
pay back David S.

    and the rest goes to my funeral.

Give my car to Jerry
& Chuck, and the rest of
my stuff they can split
    up.

What Churches Can Do

In speaking to ministers and to church groups, I have often been asked, "What can the church do to help prevent suicide?" My first response is, "Be the church." Simplistic though it may sound at first, some of the most powerful suicide prevention will be done by the church just doing what it ought to do as the church. From the New Testament book of Acts we know that the church is to preach the good news of Jesus (*kerygma*), teach and equip the believers (*didache*), and be a fellowshiping community (*koinonia*). We fail to realize sometimes the power in good worship services, strong Bible teaching and training, and the gathering together of brothers and sisters in Christ.

Second, inform the church workers about the motivations of suicidal persons, the signs of suicide, and the sources for help. Again, this is based on the understanding that the front line of defense against suicide is those persons who are regularly coming in contact with persons who may be suicidal.

Third, seek a variety of ways to equip the congregation in caregiving. I am convinced that although this is not everyone's spiritual gift, all persons can be trained in the basics of care-giving.

Fourth, get the salt out of the shaker. We as Christians are to be the salt of the world. But we need to get out there to be that salt. Encourage your church either to work with existing ministries in the community or to begin some ministries to hurting persons. I am delighted that every week our church members are working through community and Christian agencies to help the poor, battered women, the dying, the illiterate, those in jails and prisons, and the mentally ill. Each act of caring puts another roadblock in someone's path of despair that might have led to suicide.

The Continuing Role of Supporter/Friend

Returning now to your personal role as supporter/friend, even when your family member or friend is in counseling and seems to be doing better, your part in the prevention of his suicide is not over. He still needs your support and friendship.

One of the most important things you can do is stay in touch. Call and arrange times to be together to talk and some times just to do something together. Be aware of the person's schedule. A friend of mine was close to a young man who had attempted suicide. Some weeks after the attempt, Jim called the friend at work just to visit. The secretary told him his friend had not shown up for work that day. Jim called his home. There was no answer. Jim left work and went to the friend's home. The knock on the door was answered with an eerie silence. Jim got into the house and found the friend unconscious with an empty bottle of pills next to the bed. He called the emergency medical squad, and the friend's life was saved. Jim had made a commitment to stay in touch.

By staying in touch, I mean both literally and figuratively. The touch of a hand, a hug, an arm around the shoulder can be a powerful message of support at a time like this. Listen to the words of a fifty-seven-year-old man in the depths of depression:

> Beside me, my wife stirred, then reached out a hand that groped for me. She felt my shaking shoulders and suddenly came wide awake. I lifted my head to look at her and, for the first time, she saw my face as it had been through all those fear-torn nights of recent months when I had lain alone in the attic room, away from her and our Connecticut home because of work. Without a word, she took my head into her arms and

rocked it on her breast while the tears flowed on and on until it seemed my soul was pouring out of my eyes. That was the moment I have to thank for the fact that I am still alive: that moment when I was rocked and loved and comforted like the baby I had become.[8]

Awesome is the power of touch in the midst of fright and despair.

You can also be a friend by strengthening the suicidal person's support system. Involve other friends and family members with him. Reengage him in neglected activities—hobbies, recreation, and trips. Help him rediscover his spiritual resources such as prayer, Bible study with other Christians, and involvement with a committed group of caring Christians.

With adolescents a special degree of openness is required that invites them to be involved with you and to talk openly about their feelings, frustrations, and fears. Here also simply staying in touch is crucial. One mother whose teenage son took his life has this advice for parents:

I thought of him as some kind of adult and stopped watching closely what was happening in his life. I would tell parents to watch what their kids eat, what time they get in at night, what time they go to bed, how things are at school, if they get into fights, and if there is some kind of erratic behavior.

This form of careful attention must be carried out without seeming to be a watchdog or guard, but it is no less important.

In the Old Testament an important ritual was the passing of the father's blessing to the child. Many children go through life never feeling the "blessing" of their parents. Have you given your children your blessing in a way that says, "I love you, believe in you, accept you, and support you"? This blessing occurs both directly and indirectly, verbally and nonverbally. Two powerful books on this subject of conveying the blessing are Myron Madden's *The Power to Bless* (Broadman) and *The Blessing* by Gary Smalley and John Trent (Nelson).

Sam Rayburn, the late Speaker of the U.S. House of Representatives, long remembered the blessing of his father. In 1900 when Rayburn was eighteen years old, he asked his father, a North Texas farmer, for permission to leave the farm to go to college. The old man, though hating to lose the farm labor of another son, agreed, though he did not have the money to help his son attend college.

Rayburn long remembered and often recounted the day his father hitched up the buggy and took him to the train station to leave for school. With silence until the train arrived, the elder Rayburn suddenly pressed twenty-five dollars into the hand of his son.

> Sam never forgot that; he talked about that twenty-five dollars until the end of his life. "God knows how he saved it," he would say. "He never had any extra money. We earned just enough to live. It broke me up, him handing me that twenty-five dollars. I often wondered what he did without, what sacrifice he and my mother made." And he never forgot the four words his father said to him as he climbed aboard the train; he was to tell friends that he had remembered them at every crisis in his life. Clutching his son's hand, his father said: "Sam, be a man!"[9]

For young Sam Rayburn, that was the blessing that propelled him through a long and distinguished career. Your blessing will take its own unique form, but it is crucial.

Especially important is your role of supporter/friend after someone experiences hospitalization for depression or attempted suicide. As the person reenters the world that formerly felt so threatening, he needs support in the midst of those threats. Often there is a reactivation of the former feelings of depression, despair, and fright. Do not shy away because you do not know what to say or fear you will say the wrong thing. Even without mentioning the suicide thoughts or attempts, your presence can convey acceptance and love. Do not assume either that the threat of suicide is gone just because the person has received professional help and seems to be better. If you begin to see signs of regression, contact the medical team immediately to let them know what you fear may be happening.

Above all, be patient. There may even be some recurrences of the suicidal thoughts, and there may be another attempt. This does not mean that the situation is hopeless, nor does it mean that the person will never get better. It means that the problem has not run its course and more help is needed. Part of that help is your faithful standing with the person.

Also, if you are a family member or close friend, be ready to be a part of the therapeutic process as you and/or your family seek counseling to deal with the "system" in which this person lives. The suicidal process involves many people, and often those closest to the suicidal person need help, too. Willingness to get that help is one more step in the prevention of suicide and can be one more way of saying, "I love you."

Helping the Chronically Suicidal

In 1973, as part of my doctoral work while in seminary, I worked as a chaplain at Central State Hospital just outside Louisville, Kentucky. Here is one writer's description of that hospital:

Central State has dark-red brick buildings set back from the LaGrange Road on acreage that is the stuff of country clubs; the land is almost a mockery of the pain locked inside the buildings. The corridors echo with wailing. In the adult units, patients line the halls in dumb silence or pace to the beat of their own demonic drummers. The pathos is most acute in the children's unit, where young lives are sidetracked by emotional illness, often permanently.[10]

In that children's unit for two years in the early 1970s worked a young woman who took some of what she saw there and, with a determination to tell the story of "the little people"—children and adults—she'd encountered, began to write plays. One of those plays, " 'night, Mother," won a Pulitzer Prize, played on Broadway, and then was made into a movie.

" 'night, Mother" is about Jessie Cates, a woman in her thirties, whose life has gone sour and who now lives with her mother in a small house in middle America. Early in the play, Jessie tells her mother rather off-handedly that she is going to kill herself. For the next ninety minutes, the audience watches as Jessie step by step walks toward the self-determined end of her life. And her mother tries in all the ways she knows to stop her daughter from choosing death. But it is finally to no avail.

I bring this up at this point because Thelma, Jessie Cates' mother, was in the position that you may be in now. You are doing everything you know to do to stop your friend or family member from committing suicide. But sadly some persons remain suicidal for years. They are the chronically suicidal. And they are some of the most difficult people to help.

What do you do if your friend/family member just seems determined in his choice of suicide in spite of all your efforts, professional help, medication, and everything else that has been done?

Earlier I encouraged you to be patient. Your patience will be sorely tested by the chronically suicidal. For one thing, you have to bear the burden of the person's obsession with self and his or her apparent selfishness. Do not expect automatically to receive gratitude for your friendship and love because your family member/friend, under the circumstances, may not be forthcoming with either. I do believe, however, that we should not too easily excuse such behavior. We should teach people how to treat us, and depression is no excuse for one person using or abusing another. The depressed/suicidal person needs a network of supportive people. Ingratitude only alienates needed friends. Therefore, in subtle and direct ways encourage and insist that your friend/family member recognize the help being given.

But your patience may be so sorely tested that you probably will get to the place that you do even wish in a moment of anger he would go ahead and take his life. You may think, *If he's going to be so miserable and make everyone else miserable, let him do it!*

In this tough situation, do what you can do, and keep praying that the person will come to a point of re-decision where he chooses life instead of death. Set limits as best you can about amount and frequency of time with the person or you will soon become drained, frustrated, and angry. If this is a spouse, parent, or child, make a concerted effort to keep living your life/pursuing your career and interests. You do this in part to keep from being dragged down to a death-like life that the suicidal person is living.

Keep trying to maintain a network of persons around the individual, although that does become hard because people do not like to be around depressed people. Depression is contagious, after all. That is why you need as many positive people and things around you as possible.

Remember, what you say to the chronically suicidal person is important. But even more important than what you *say* is who you *are* to the person.

One of the most taxing things about maintaining a relationship with the chronically suicidal, though, is what and how much he wants to say to you. Although most people, when depressed, withdraw, some want to talk incessantly about themselves and their depression. Be cautious about this. You reach a point of diminishing returns where more talking about it is not doing the individual any good. Also, depression is contagious and getting caught in this obsession with depressive thoughts can drag you down and sap you of the energy you need both to cope personally and to help the suicidal person. In addition, unless you put limits on the person's talking, you will most likely either withdraw or lash out in anger.

Another question that is sometimes asked is, "Should you always treat the suicidal person with kid gloves?" I say no. You need to be loving and supportive, but sometimes the most loving thing to do is to confront the person. You generally want to avoid such hackneyed phrases as "You need to just snap out of it" or "Just pull yourself together and get going again." But there do come times when supportive becomes coddling and loving becomes excuse-making. You have a right to be confrontive at times and a right to express frustration. You certainly have a right to call the person to responsibility. Obviously it always needs to be done with the backing of love and concern. I know all this is not easy.

I do not mean to put too heavy a load on your shoulders, but your firm stance against suicide may be *the* thing that keeps this person from completing the suicide. Therefore, even if you become resigned to the fact that your friend/family member may remain depressed/suicidal for years, be on guard against coming to the place of saying, "Well, it is inevitable and there is nothing I can do. I am not going to stand in his way." There are plenty of instances documented in which a suicidal person sensed that resignation and took it as "permission" to end his life.

What I am saying is that you stand as a sentinel on guard against the enemy, suicide. Sometimes it is lonely duty and sometimes you wonder if your watch will ever be over. There are times when being able to rest in sleep seems so much more inviting than the watchful eye. But there are times in the lives of some people when the enemy, suicide, seems ever alert and ready to strike. It has been often said, "The price of liberty is eternal vigilance." To paraphrase, "One of the prices of friendship with a chronically suicidal person is eternal vigilance."

Conclusion

Can you really help prevent the suicide of a person close to you? Yes. You cannot do it alone and there are limits to what you can do, but you may be the most important person in the process of suicide prevention for another person. Because that is a demanding task, you will need help. The following chapter is designed as a guide to your feelings in this process and to the assistance you need in order to be an effective helper.

5

To Help, Do I Need Help?

IF THE PRIMARY MEANS of preventing suicide is the relationship you have with the suicidal person, then it stands to reason that you should pay attention to your own needs and feelings. Your ability to relate effectively to the suicidal person depends on a certain objectivity on your part, attention to personal dynamics, the support of family, friends, and faith, and the possible assistance of professionals.

Dealing with suicide is such a demanding situation that far too many people become centered on the possibility of suicide and lose perspective on the larger picture of what is occurring. Part of the loss of perspective results from failure to see how you "fit into the picture." Another temptation is to become so self-giving that you cause the suicidal person to become overdependent on you. There are times when we may choose to allow the person to become temporarily dependent, but that dependence must be carefully monitored and skillfully decreased as soon as possible.

Suicide is a cry for help. The poignancy of that cry calls forth in most of us, at least initially, a tremendous desire "to do something." We may become very quickly involved with a person after a suicide attempt only to realize later how demanding and confusing that situation can become. In fact, in a very short time we can feel that our resources, patience, and skills are exhausted and we are "drawing from an empty well." In that case it is important to take some steps to gain a perspective and get help for ourselves. Is this selfish? No more so than were Jesus' periodic retreats for times of solitude and prayer and his temporary withdrawal from the crowds to be with his small band of disciples. In our lives, as in Jesus', there are times for talking and times for silence, times for action and times for reflection, times for being present and times for being absent.

This chapter deals with some of the feelings most commonly reported by persons close to suicidal family members and friends. Having looked at these feelings, attention will then be given to specific steps to take to get the help you may need for yourself.

Dealing with Your Feelings

1. Guilt

When suicide is threatened, attempted, or completed, one of the most common feelings engendered is guilt. "Why didn't I care more?" "Why was I so thoughtless and insensitive?" "I feel terrible because I didn't take him seriously." "If I had been the father/mother/husband/wife/child/sibling/friend I should be, this never would have happened."

Sometimes the guilt is justified. More often it is based on magical thinking which implies that if only one thing had been done or said, all this would not have happened. This kind of magical thinking fails to recognize suicide as a process that takes from weeks to years to develop.

The fact that suicide threats and attempts induce guilt in those around is usually no real surprise to the threatener or attempter. In fact, it is important for us to know what our guilt motivates us to do for the suicidal person that he or she wanted us to do. What are they requesting from us by their action? Having answered that, we can understand better our response to what has happened. Sometimes the request is a legitimate one, even though the form of the request is inadequate. If a teenage daughter is saying to her busy mother, "Pay attention to me! Listen to me!", her request may be entirely understandable. If a wife's attempt is a cry to be considered seriously and not taken for granted, then that request deserves attention. Likewise an attempt by an employee may be a way of saying, "Relieve me of some of this stress."

Legitimate though some requests may be, in the rush of the immediate moment, we must be careful about over-promising what we will do. Too often promises are made that will not or cannot be kept. Then anger and distance result. At times a vicious cycle is set up in which, after a suicide attempt is made, the situation changes dramatically, with the attempter receiving much attention, only to lose that attention as things return to "normal." In a somewhat infantile way, the suicidal person then attempts suicide again so he can get what he wants and was perhaps promised. The tragic reality is that, to have effect, the attempts must become more dramatic and hence more lethal.

Consider also that some requests made by suicide threats and attempts are not legitimate. Can a teenage boy refuse to break up with his girlfriend because she has made an attempt? Can a young wife stay with an abusive husband she is planning to divorce because he threatens suicide? Can an employer refuse to demote a worker because he threatens suicide? These threats must be taken seriously, but the reality is that if our guilt motivates us to give in to unreasonable demands, we have not resolved the problem. We have only postponed the crisis and set up an inadequate pattern of relating.

There is also the guilt that comes when one finds oneself wishing the person would go ahead and take his life. This is especially present when repeated attempts have been made, the depression lingers for years, or it seems that the mental illness will always be present. Rather than castigate yourself for these feelings, seek a mature friend or counselor with whom to talk out these feelings. This should be done lest you even indirectly send out the message, "Go ahead."

2. Fear

Following a suicide attempt or threat, fear fills the air. First, there is fear if the attempt or threat "came out of the blue without warning." Many times family members are completely surprised by an attempt or a suicide. They report that as far as they knew everything was fine, and they had no idea their family member was so desperate or depressed. The surprise and suddenness strike fear in the hearts of those close to the suicidal person.

Second, now knowing that this person has come close to carrying out suicide, the question becomes, "Will he try again?" Following an attempt, there is the desire to watch every move the person makes and never let him be alone lest he complete what he earlier attempted.

Third, fear haunts family members and friends with the possibility that "I may say or do something that will cause him to suicide." This results in everyone "walking on egg shells" or completely avoiding the person as a way of getting protection from being the "cause" of a suicide. Also, it inhibits expressions of feeling, especially anger. Though angry with the person who has attempted or talked about suicide, you fear expressing that anger lest it be the very thing that triggers the suicidal thoughts.

Fourth, there may be some fear that your family member or friend will turn his violence not only toward himself but also toward you or someone else. Less than four percent of the suicides in the United States are preceded by murder. That is small comfort, though, when we continue to read about murder-suicides. If you have any reason to believe that such a possibility exists with your family member or friend, this should be discussed immediately with his counselor/therapist or another responsible person.

Fifth, fear may arise when suicide comes close because we are afraid that we will take the same path. Most persons have had at least fleeting suicidal thoughts. When the issue of suicide is raised by the attempt of someone close to you, those thoughts may become more than fleeting. If they do, immediately seek out a trusted friend or counselor to talk with about those thoughts.

Sixth, particularly following a completed suicide but also after an attempt, there may be some fear that suicide is some kind of disease which you or other family members may "catch." This may especially be a concern of children in the family. This should be talked out with the emphasis on the individual nature of suicide and with reassurance that suicide is not a disease which "attacks" people leaving them helpless to resist.

3. Hurt

In part, a suicide threat or attempt is a rejection of those closest to the person. Family members can interpret a suicide or attempt as the person saying, "I'd rather be dead than living with you." That rejection hurts. We may feel that it says we were inadequate as a parent, spouse, sibling, lover, child, partner, or friend. There can also be feelings of hurt because the love that person has for us was not strong enough to keep him from considering suicide. The irony of this is that some persons attempt suicide as an "expression of love" as they "rid" the family of a "burden."

Some persons respond to the hurt they feel by withdrawing from the suicidal person. Because of the rejection they feel, they in turn reject the other. Sometimes that withdrawal and rejection is a form of anticipatory grief. It is like saying, "Even though you did not take your life this time, by pulling away from you I'm going to protect myself from being hurt."

Though there may be a temptation to withdraw from the suicidal person, this can be devastating to him. In fact, at times the person making a suicide attempt does so as a way to test the love of those around him. When he experiences their withdrawal and rejection, his worst fears are "confirmed"—"They really didn't love me."

Another form the hurt may take is the response based on the notion that the specific intent of the attempted suicide was to hurt you. "How could you do this to me?" is a response of some to a suicide attempt. Though this may be just what you are wondering, to ask such a question implies that your concern is more with yourself than with the attempter. If you sense that the attempt was in fact a hostile gesture toward you, this feeling will need to be explored sometime, but immediately the person who has made the attempt needs to know of your concern for him. For you to say by your actions that even a suicide attempt will not destroy your love and concern for the person is a powerful reminder that his ill-considered action will not produce rejection in you.

It should be noted here that although suicide is often perceived by the survivors as rejection, when you examine the complexity of motivations for suicide, you realize that often it is not in fact a rejection of loved ones. The pain can be so intense or the distorted perspective of suicide has so taken over that the suicidal person sees no other way out. In fact he may feel that his suicide is a gesture of love. Suicide can be a terrible form of rejection, but it is not always intended as that.

4. Anger

The anger engendered by a suicide attempt or a serious threat is frequently a secondary emotion to the guilt that is felt. But the anger is still there. That anger comes from many sources.

Sometimes the anger is caused by the embarrassment and trouble that may have been caused. The anger can result from how stupidly or immaturely you feel the person has acted. At a deeper level, your anger may come from the realization of the tremendous grief that you would have had if the attempt had been successful or the threat carried out. There is rather considerable anger when you feel the person was "running out on you" and leaving you to pick up the pieces and to carry on the responsibilities he had shirked. This anger can be seen, for instance, in the husband who would have been left to care for three young children had his wife's attempt been successful.

When promises are broken, anger is inevitable. Suicide breaks promises. Marriage explicitly or implicitly brings the promise of a reasonably happy and full life together. When one of the couple commits suicide, those promises are not kept. The child who attempts or completes suicide is often described as being a "special" or exceptional child. These descriptions imply the promise of great things to come. When a suicide attempt is made, all those promises of the future are called into question. They do not seem to mean to the child what they mean to the parent.

What do you do with these feelings of anger? You feel that you have to treat a person with kid gloves after he has attempted suicide, and yet your anger is still with you.

First, you can share these feelings with a friend you trust who will not feel the need to give you a lot of advice. What you need is someone who will just listen. Commit these concerns to God in prayer and seek the guidance of the Spirit about how they should be dealt with. At some later time you may come to the place that you are ready to talk out your feelings of anger directly with the suicidal person. If that is done, be straightforward without being cutting or unkind. Be specific, assure him of your love, and remind him that he is responsible for his behavior. If the person is still in therapy, you would be well advised to talk with his therapist prior to this confrontation or do it in a session with the therapist present.

5. Helplessness

You may feel helpless as you attempt to talk to a family member or friend who is suicidal. For one thing, each alternative you suggest may be met with a "Yes, but—" answer. Nothing you propose seems to be reasonable or appealing to the person. Also, your sense of helplessness may be heightened by the circular logic used by some suicidal persons. The irrationality and faulty reasoning of some suicidal persons leaves us confused and frustrated.

Helplessness may become a strong feeling when you realize fully that if this person firmly resolves to take his life, in the final analysis you cannot prevent him. Is this to deny all that this book has been about? No. There is much you can do to prevent suicide, but when a person has a very strong commitment to kill himself, with little ambivalence, suicide prevention takes herculean efforts. Even then, the most well-trained hospital staff can fail in their attempt to prevent such a death. Most suicides can be prevented. Some cannot.

A word of caution should be spoken here. A number of studies have indicated that the chance of suicide occurring is increased if the response to the suicidal person is characterized by helplessness and hopelessness. Why is that? Because the person considering suicide is already feeling helpless and hopeless. If he sees the same thing in the person to whom he is reaching out for help, then his own worst fears are confirmed. Therefore, though you may feel helpless, try to convey a sense of power and being in control. This show of strength can provide new hope for the suicidal person that perhaps things can change for the better.

When you have listened carefully to the dilemmas and problems of a person considering suicide, you may get the feeling that there is no hope. Do not give in to the feeling that there is no hope. Do not give in to this feeling lest the other person sink lower in his despair. It is false to respond with a naïve Pollyanna attitude or a mindless positive-thinking approach, but for the Christian there is always hope based on the realization of the nature of God and his love for us. Despair is the absence of hope, but for the Christian, hope is always present. Draw from that reservoir of hope even when things look hopeless. Remember that your attitude is based not just on the person's reaction or your response to him, but on the hope you have for the working of the Spirit of God in this situation.

6. Frustration

The sense of helplessness and the confusion engendered by the seeming irrationality of the suicidal person lead to feelings of frustration. You are frustrated by your seeming inability to help significantly, and by the mixture of feelings you may be experiencing.

Again, a friend is needed to help you sort out these feelings. This needs to be a person who will let you "blow off steam," and who will not demand that everything you say be logical or that every feeling you have be justified. I realize that such friends are rare. If you do not already have one, try to find one, or "buy" one by paying to see a good counselor/therapist.

The alternatives to having such a friend who can be a sounding board for your feelings and thoughts are (1) to bottle up inside you the frustration and/or (2) to lash out in anger or desperation at the suicidal person. Unfortunately, some suicidal persons are waiting for just such a blow-up to give them the "permission" to go ahead and kill themselves. This kind of suicide is a form of the "You'll-be-sorry" game or "Look-what-you-made-me-do" game or "Now-I've-got-you" game.

7. Discouragement

Discouragement comes easily if the person who is suicidal remains depressed, continues to threaten, or keeps attempting suicide.

Discouragement leads to hopelessness and can result in depression. "Why keep him from trying if he is going to do it anyway?" you may ask yourself. "If he really is this miserable and wants to die this much, should I keep him from it?" "Nothing I do seems to work anyway; why not just quit trying?"

You do not quit trying because this is a person of worth created in the image of God who is about to destroy what God has created. But in the midst of discouragement that thought can seem unrealistically ethereal and philosophical. It is no less true, however.

Discouragement may sometimes result from discontinuing the treatment if the person is under the care of a professional. At this point some families take the person out of the hospital even against medical advice. Why do they do this? Because they see no marked improvement and perhaps it even seems that the person is getting worse. Also, they may feel they are wasting money if they do not think their family member or friend is getting better. Sometimes, sadly, the person is taken out of the hospital almost in a "Let's-take-him-home-to-die" attitude, though this is usually subconscious.

Be extremely cautious about taking a suicidal person out of counseling or out of a hospital, even, and especially, when the crisis seems to have passed. Remember that the three months after a depression are some of the highest times of suicide risk. Also, remember that this person did not become suicidal overnight, and you cannot expect him to "pull out of it" overnight. In fact, if he gets better very fast, be extremely cautious and attentive because he may be just gaining the energy to do what he earlier only contemplated or half-heartedly attempted.

This word of caution does not mean, however, that you uncritically accept the reports of the professional person working with your family member or friend. Continue to express interest, get reports, ask questions, and, if the person is hospitalized, visit often unless the staff requests that for a limited time you not see the patient. Even when you cannot see the patient, keep in touch with the professional staff. (A word of advice: If you do not get your questions answered by the patient's medical doctor, talk to some of the rest of the staff, such as a psyciatric social worker, nurse, or chaplain. They are often quite helpful.)

More will be said in the second part of this chapter about some steps to take that will aid in dealing with discouragement.

8. Shame

Shame is the emotion connected to the fear of what others will think. We are ashamed personally when something happens in which we have violated our own perception of "our best self" and others' perception of us. In other words, we are remorseful in part because we feel we have been less than we should be and have thereby done wrong.

When a family member or close friend attempts suicide, the shame may result from your sense of having failed to do what you feel you should have done to prevent the suicidal person from attempting to take his life. The shame may be more closely tied to a concern about what others will think. "Will they think I am a bad parent?" "Will they think I didn't love him enough?" "Will they ever be our friends again?" "Will they think our family is crazy?"

Although in many cultures suicide is not looked upon as something to be ashamed of, in most of western culture it has been. For many centuries in Europe, the body of a person who committed suicide would be exhibited for public ridicule, all property would be confiscated, and the deceased was not permitted to be buried in the common burial ground of the community.

Though we no longer treat the person who has suicided nor his family in such a brutish manner, in our society suicide remains in most circles and in most circumstances a shameful way to die. Therefore, when a suicide attempt is made, some of the questions we torture ourselves with are, in fact, being asked by others.

Some will react judgmentally and self-righteously. Many will draw the wrong conclusions. Some will turn detective, seeking to find out "what really happened and why." Others will suddenly become junior psychiatrists analyzing and diagnosing the person and the family. Fortunately, there are some who will not pluralize judgment and will be there to listen, support, and help.

There is little we can do about other people's reactions to a suicide attempt or threat. We do not have control over their reactions. What we do have control over is our response to the event and to the individual. As Victor Frankl noted in the Nazi concentration camps of World War II, our ultimate freedom is to choose our attitude toward what is happening to us.

One of your responses to a suicide attempt or threat may be shame because you sense that your family is somehow a failure. The decision of one member of the family that he no longer wants to live is a fairly powerful challenge to the image of your family as happy and healthy.

If you are a Christian and your family is active in church, the shame may be even more intensely felt. Many Christians have the idea that if you are a Christian family, you will not have problems. This is reinforced in many churches by idealistic and romantic notions of the family presented from the pulpit and in Bible study sessions. This mistaken notion is furthered by active church families trying desperately to keep up the image of the nice, happy, problem-free family.

The teaching of the gospel does not maintain that you will have no problems as a family if all of you are Christians. The teaching of the gospel is that you have Jesus Christ as your special resource for dealing with the problems that inevitably come up in any family!

Relieve the pressure on your family by not demanding perfection. The intense desire and strained effort of having a happy family that never disagrees, argues, or gets distant from one another is a bigger burden than families can bear.

9. Anxiety

Suicide creates anxiety. In his book on adolescent suicide, Andre Haim claimed, "Suicide arouses a more acute anxiety than any other kind of death, and triggers off even more intense reactions of defense and rejection."[1]

Why all this anxiety? Surely there are many reasons, but let us look at a few.

First, suicide raises the questions, sometimes only slightly, "Was this person right? Is life not worth living? Is death better?" Even when we may not have thought about it consciously, we keep going in part by believing that life is worth living. If it were not, then our existence would be absurd and a major barrier to suicide would have toppled. A suicide or attempt close by raises the question for us in a dramatic way.

Second, a suicide or near suicide kicks up our own death anxiety. Again, though it may not be conscious, each of us has some anxiety about dying. The fear of nonexistence and the uncertainty about what lies beyond death's door—yes, even for a Christian— breeds anxiety.

Third, if the person who has attempted suicide is your child, then their near-death has threatened your future. A child is a way we have of continuing to live. In the ancient Hebrew tradition, having children was a way of surviving death. When death came, if children survived you, then a part of you had not died. Also, when a child attempts suicide, he has almost destroyed his future about which you have so many hopes, not the least of those hopes being seeing some of your own dreams realized through your children.

Daniel J. Levinson and his colleagues note this in *The Seasons of a Man's Life.* They observe that "the joys and despondencies parents feel in middle age often seem excessive. The parents' preoccupations with 'how the children are doing' make more sense when seen in the context of the legacy: They reflect basic feelings about the value of one's contribution to posterity and one's claim on immorality."[2]

Fourth, if a child, a sibling, or a mate attempts suicide, then a part of you almost died. Tennyson was right when he wrote in the poem "Ulysses," "I am a part of all that I have met." A close family member is even more a part of you because of blood or adoptive ties.

I well remember as a pastor talking with two persons each of whom was a twin. One woman's twin had committed suicide and the other's twin had attempted it. The anxiety was very high because each had a poignant and sacred sense that a part of her had died or almost died. This is testimony to the caution that should be exercised with the surviving twin when his sibling has taken his life or attempted to do so. With twins, there is such a bond that the suicide of one beckons the other down the same road. It can seem as if because they have been, in a sense, one all their lives, they ought to be in death.

Fifth, the anxiety is heightened around a suicide attempt if someone close to you has previously completed suicide.

When a general feeling of anxiety continues over several weeks or if it becomes acute anxiety, professional help should be sought as soon as possible. This anxiety may take somatic forms such as backache or other muscle tension, constipation, headache, indigestion, lack of concentration, or sleep disturbance.

10. Depression

Some studies indicate that depression is more prevalent in families of suicidal persons. Why is that? All the answers are not in, but these studies do bear out what is often reported as the "feeling tone" of many families where suicide occurs or attempts are made.

Is depression contagious? Yes, ask any counselor who sees several depressed clients in one day. After a while, the counselor begins to become depressed! To be around someone who has very little energy, is down emotionally, and is raising questions about the meaninglessness of life is to make ourselves vulnerable to becoming depressed. Also, if depression and suicide attempts have persisted over a long time, discouragement on your part may lead to depression.

Obviously, if you find yourself getting stuck in a depressed state, you should seek competent help. Get that help before you get so deep in depression that you do not have the energy to reach out.

The Help You Need

Reading through the list and explanations of feelings associated with suicide and suicide attempts, you may feel a bit overwhelmed and wonder how capable you are of giving significant help to a suicidal person.

Your ability to help a suicidal person is dependent on your ability to maintain perspective, to sustain your equilibrium, and to marshal the forces of personal coping that are available to you. In other words, to help in the midst of this suicidal crisis you have to take care of yourself.

One of the primary needs of anyone working with suicidal persons is a sense of power. This power is both the ability to take action and the emotional energy required to function well in a crisis. It is neither autocratic nor manipulative power; instead, it is a power that grows out of concern and love. This power is based in a sense of our worth before God as one of his creatures. True humility characterizes this power, because true humility involves a realistic sense of both our strengths and our weaknesses, our limitations and our abilities.

But, you ask, where do we get this sense of power so needed in working with suicidal persons? We get it through the qualities identified in the acronym SEKS. That acronym sounds more exciting when spoken than it does when read. Nevertheless, I have become convinced that the factors those four letters stand for are essential to a sense of power. The four are Spirit, exercise, knowledge, and support.

1. Spirit

By "Spirit," I mean God's Holy Spirit. God's Holy Spirit resides in every believer and every believer can be filled with the Spirit. The Holy Spirit, one expression of the Holy Trinity, is essentially a minister, a guide, a convicter, a comforter to us. In John 14:18 when Jesus promised to send the Spirit, he said, "When I go, you will not be left all alone; I will come back to you" (TEV). We are not alone! God's Spirit is at work in us!

If we are going to have spiritual power, then it will come as we open ourselves to God working in and through us by his Spirit. For you see, in this situation, as in all situations, God has created us as free moral agents. We are free to choose. We can choose to permit the ministry of the Spirit in our lives, or we can refuse to allow God's Spirit to do his work through us. We can even harden our hearts and ignore the convicting work of the Spirit which leads to salvation. We can refuse God's offer of salvation. That is the unpardonable sin.

This may sound rather theoretical and abstract when you are desperately seeking to keep a daughter or a husband or a friend from completing an earlier suicide attempt. Believe me, though, this kind of spiritual power is crucial to your being a significant help to this family member or friend. You need the power of God working with you in this situation. That power is available.

Jennifer was sixteen when her relationship with her mother seemed to be at its worst. Jennifer was the middle child, with an older sister and a younger brother. In what was almost a classic fashion, Jennifer found herself caught between an outstanding older sister and a younger brother who seemed to be the apple of the family's eye.

Beginning in middle school, Jennifer seemed to drift farther and farther away from her family. Not until much later did her mother realize that the drift and the delinquent behavior Jennifer got into was an attempt to get attention. It was also an attempt to test how much her mother loved her. Jennifer's question seemed to be, "Will you still love me even when I disappoint you?" She was seeking rejection but desperately wanted to be accepted so she would know she was loved—even though she was not outstanding like her older sister or as "lovable" as her younger brother.

One way to see how much she was loved was to attempt suicide. On her sixteenth birthday, Jennifer took an overdose of pills and lay down on the living room couch "to sleep." After coming in from work, her mother tried to awaken her for supper. Jennifer was groggy and reluctantly told her mother what she had done. Her mother called a friend, they took Jennifer to the hospital, her stomach was pumped, and she was admitted for observation. Counseling followed, but Jennifer held to her option of suicide. Her delinquent behavior continued.

Some weeks later, Jennifer's mother, distraught and frightened, awoke early. She got out of bed, began reading her Bible, and had a long time of prayer. She especially prayed for patience and a sense of power, because she seemed weak and discouraged. Through the prayer time, God seemed to be telling her to reach out to Jennifer again, that morning, with a reassurance of love.

After breakfast, as Jennifer was in her room getting dressed and ready for school, her mother stopped by the room, leaned against the door frame, and said, "Jenny, I don't know why you've been going through all the things you have, but I want you to know that there's nothing you can do to make me stop loving you." With that, Jennifer's mother slowly walked away. Somehow these were the words that turned Jennifer's life around. She knew in that moment that her mother was not going to reject her. She knew that her mother loved her and always would. She gave up her notions of suicide and began to "come back" to her family.

How do you explain the power of those words? Surely at another time or to another child, they would have been taken as a challenge, not as acceptance. I believe they can be explained by the power of God and by the Spirit guiding Jennifer's mother.

How do you appropriate and use the power experienced by Jennifer's mother? You do so by opening yourself to God and asking for his help through the guidance of his Spirit. Even if you have not been regular or even occasional in prayer, you can pray openly to God. God does not require fancy, "correct" prayers. He asks for honest, heartfelt prayers. Open your life to God in prayer and invite him to fill your life with his Spirit. Allow yourself to sense and draw upon the presence and the power of God's Spirit in you. Now daily commit yourself to an openness to God's Spirit and a daily communion with God through prayer.

The presence of God's Spirit is not always evidenced in dramatic ways. More often it is the subtle and quiet power that keeps us going through the roughest of times and gives us hope in the face of seemingly overwhelming obstacles.

Realize that the God who created all that is, who sustains his creation even this very moment, who will one day bring all of creation to fulfillment—that same God is ready to be Friend, Guide, Comforter through his Spirit. That is a gift beyond measure and it is available to you! When you stand with your suicidal family member or friend, you do not stand alone! God is with you.

2. Exercise

What does exercise have to do with coping with a suicidal crisis? It has more effect than you might think.

Increasingly, counselors who work with depressed persons or persons susceptible to depression are taking a more wholistic approach in their counseling. Not only is the problem "talked out," but also it is worked out by recommendations about living conditions, daily schedule, diet, and *exercise.* Several recent studies have indicated that vigorous exercise increases the production of certain chemicals in the brain that are natural antidepressants. In addition, vigorous exercise can be a stress-reducer. It gives you an increased sense of power as you become better conditioned. And it can provide recreation if it is not just seen as another task to be done.

What does this have to do with you? If you are working with a suicidal person and especially if this person may remain suicidal over a long period of time, you need the sense of power that comes from proper diet and exercise. As a by-product, if you can get the other person to join you in this exercise, you will have taken a significant step toward preventing his suicide.

3. Knowledge

In the sixteenth century, Francis Bacon declared, "Knowledge is power." That statement still holds.

But what kind of power are we talking about in the context of this book? I identify three facets, the first of which is self-knowledge. Socrates' dictum, "Know thyself," remains a wise word to us. Because of the power of personal relationships in preventing suicide, our personhood becomes an instrument of suicide prevention. But without self-knowledge, that instrument is less effective. Far from the morbid introspection that examines the motives behind every action, this self-knowledge is in touch with and aware of past history and how that has shaped us. But it is also aware of present feelings and responses, for true self-knowledge is based on self-awareness and self-acceptance. This self-knowledge involves awareness of our limitations and our strengths. With self-knowledge we recognize our natural down times and the natural high times. Self-knowledge enables an accurate appraisal of our needs for support and who can provide that needed support.

General knowledge is another important element of personal power. In the midst of dealing with a suicidal crisis, we need not only spiritual and physical strength, but also mental stability. A foundation of general knowledge prepares us for thinking (which seems almost a dying art among Americans) and for the kind of reading and conversation that provide mental stimulation—a surprising source of strength as well as needed diversion.

The third element of knowledge/power is the strength that comes from specific knowledge about suicide, its nature and its prevention. The very fact that you are now operating from good information about suicide instead of myths adds to your resources for dealing adequately with the situation.

4. Support

The fourth source of power available to you, the helper, in this crisis is the power of support. Even as isolation, emotional and physical, increases the chance of suicide in the person you are trying to help, so isolation decreases the chances of your being an effective preventer of suicide.

How isolated are you from family, friends, and other sources of support? Are there people around you with whom you feel comfortable to share your feelings honestly and openly? If not, then you need to begin building a support system.

Where do you start? I believe there are four primary sources: faith, family, friends, and professional help.

(1) Faith in God who loves us, a Savior who has paid the supreme sacrifice for us, and a Spirit that ministers to us and through us can be the greatest support of all. That faith support is activated by a trustful, open response to God, a commitment to regular prayer, involvement with a group of fellow believers in Bible study and worship, and a daily living out of the faith and its implications. That sounds simple and easy. In a sense it is simple, but it is never easy.

Following the death of my friend to whom this book is dedicated, I suffered a mild depression for about six weeks. Then I suddenly became more conscious of the support of my faith and specifically that the life force behind the universe was a loving God who wanted the best for his creatures. Now I find myself almost daily more aware of the color of the sky, the songs of birds, the beauty of flowers, the strength of trees, the laughter of a friend. All of these become to me reminders of God's love and support. My faith is crucial support for living.

Obviously, if you are struggling to keep afloat emotionally and perhaps are angry even at God for the crisis you find yourself in, faith as support will not come easily. I would urge you to recognize and accept the anger you feel and in prayer talk to God about those feelings. God is big enough to accept and to deal with your anger.

The support that comes from involvement in a local church can be most helpful at a time like this. Criticism about the church not doing more for our society often ignores the good the church does simply by providing opportunities for group Bible study and worship. The inspiration, fellowship, guidance, and assistance the church provides are significant and valuable aids to living in our world. Even if you have not been to church in some time, take the first step in finding a congregation where you can attend and become involved. Often people who have lived their lives outside the church or on the fringes of it, think that church-going people are sort of weird. Become involved in a church and you will soon discover that church-going people are merely people like yourself—normal human beings who have the same struggles as everyone else, but they have the strength of faith to aid them in those struggles.

(2) How much support will your family be in this crisis? Do they understand what is going on? If not, why not? Who among

the family is most helpful and who is least helpful? Who in the family can you talk to openly and know your discussion will be kept confidential?

As we will see in the next chapter, there is unbelievable complexity in the family's involvement in suicide. The reality is that some family members or a whole family can be more of a hindrance than a help in preventing the suicide of one of its own members. So, the support of family has to be looked at rather carefully. But consciously give thought to how your family can provide support for you. This support takes not only the form of understanding and conversation, but also strength simply through times together, fun times, shared meals, and diversion. Do not overlook the support of children since their perspective of the world and play with them provides hope, frivolity, and a sense of the continuation of life.

If you do not find much support coming from your family, rather than becoming immobilized and frustrated by your anger toward them, begin to seek other sources of support. One source is friends.

(3) Who are your friends? How often do you see them? How do you keep in touch with them? How many friends do you have who make you feel better about yourself when you are around them? Which friends bring out the best in you? And which ones bring out the worst?

We tend not to think consciously about our network of friends in these ways. Why? Because usually friendship just happens, and we do not give much deliberate attention to how friendships are formed and with whom. I urge you to give some attention to this.

I see three levels of friendship. The first is that core of friends with whom I can be open and honest. These are the friends with whom I can share my deepest thoughts, my dreams, my disappointments, my greatest joys, and my most profound doubts. The corollary of that is that they can do the same with me. Most of these, I find, are persons with whom I have some history; our friendship has crossed the years and our mutual trust has been nurtured. By the way, I can number those friends on the fingers of one hand. I do not say that with sadness, because I believe it is virtually impossible to have this depth of friendship with more than a few people. But those persons are crucial.

The second level of friendship includes people at work, at church, and in other settings—people I simply enjoy being with, working with, and having fun with. There is sharing here, too, but not at the depth of the first level.

The third level of friendship stretches the definition of friendship, because these are simply people with whom I have little contact and conversation, but they provide for me and I for them the "ministry of presence." These include the security guard I greet every day at work, the parking lot attendant, the bus driver, people I see at the Y, people I meet in travel, and countless other people I have social contact with. Are these friends? Yes, in the broadest sense of that word. These persons are a part of our support system, and when we become isolated or alienated from them there is a sense of loss.

What I am urging you to do is to look deliberately at all three levels of friendship and find ways to strengthen all of them. What if you do not have friends at one or all of these levels? Then begin to develop them. Consciously decide to build these friendships. How do you do that? You do it by realizing where the gaps are in your network of friends, by being a friend and by being friendly, and by seeking out people whom you would like to be friends with and finding occasions to be with them. One woman I know who was struggling with loneliness bought two season tickets to the theater and asked different friends to go with her to the plays. Other people I know have become involved in civic and political endeavors as an avenue of making new friends. But in this quest for friends do not overlook old friendships that may have been neglected.

The reality is, though, that some people make friends more easily than others. If you find this difficult, then you may need some help. I highly recommend for this purpose the wise book by Loy McGinnis, *The Friendship Factor,* or Velma Stevens's book, *A New Look at Loneliness.*

Let's face it, we all "get by with a little help from our friends." And certainly when you are trying to prevent a suicide, you need the help of friends.

(4) You may decide to "buy" the friendship of a professional. Does that sound crass? Can you ever "buy" friendship? In most senses the answer is no, but when you seek out and hire a

counselor/therapist to help you, you are in a sense buying that individual's friendship. You are buying his time, during which you will seek his expertise, perspective, and support.

In the fourth chapter and also in the next chapter, I deal with the issue of seeking professional help. So here I will be brief.

You may want to seek out a minister (for whom there is usually no fee), a psychologist, a child development specialist (usually a professor at a college or seminary), a pastoral counselor, a clinical social worker, or a psychiatrist. The fees will vary and the number of visits will depend on how much help you are seeking, the type of therapy this person uses, and his assessment of the help you need.

Because you are hiring someone to do a job for you, you should shop around by inquiring beforehand about his training, experience, professional accreditations, fees, and type of therapy. Talk with friends to find out their experiences with various counselors/therapists.

Should you see the same person that your family member or friend who is suicidal is seeing? You may choose a therapist for yourself other than this person's therapist, but you may be helped in better understanding your family member or friend by talking to his therapist. In the case of a family member, I would be suspicious of a therapist who did not involve the whole family in some way, if not in the therapy, at least in consultation.

But if you seek out this person's therapist, what can you legitimately ask him or her? First, because of the needed confidentiality, the therapist cannot tell you what is happening in the private sessions with the suicidal person. You can, however, ask for a general assessment of the person, a prediction about the amount of time and therapy that will be required, and advice on how you can be a help to the person. Do not be afraid to ask very specific questions abut what will be most helpful and what will not. Also, offer your perspective of your family member or friend. You can help the therapist be a better therapist because of your insight and perspective.

Perhaps, though, you may be asking, "Why should I seek help when it is my family member/friend who needs the help?" If you are finding yourself becoming depressed, overly anxious, extremely angry, or helpless, your ability to help this person will be diminished. To continue to be an effective part of the defense against this suicide you may need professional help to function better, to cope with the situation, and to understand how you fit into the picture.

Conclusion

To help, do you need help? Yes, and that help takes many forms and is available in numerous ways. The help is available, but it is up to you to seek it and utilize it. In his Sermon on the Mount, Jesus said, "Ask, and it will be given you; seek, and you will find; knock, and it will be opened to you." (Matt. 7:7, RSV). That is not just advice; that is a truth of life. Faced with a person who is about to destroy his life, you need help. If the suicide can be prevented and if you are going to help prevent it, ask, seek, and knock, and keep asking, seeking, and knocking for the needed help.

6

Who Is Responsible?

FOLLOWING SUICIDE there is the inevitable guilt which asks the question, "Am I responsible for this?" For family members and very close friends there is often shame which asks, "Do other people think this was my fault?" Motivating these questions is the sense of responsibility we feel for those close to us. When a suicide or attempt occurs, who is responsible?

This chapter explores the question of responsibility. First we will look at the four keys to understanding human motivation, and then we will examine the limits of our responsibility. It is my hope that after having read this chapter you will be able to maintain a healthy sense of responsibility which is aware of its limits and not over-responsible.

The Four-Legged Table of Human Motivation

What motivates people? Why do we do the things we do? Are we just pawns of fate or chemically controlled robots and therefore not responsible for our behavior?

These questions and others like them have been asked since the creation of man. The number of different answers given very nearly equals the number of questions that have been asked. Is it presumptuous then to attempt to set out in a few pages the keys to human motivation? Perhaps so, but it is also potentially helpful. Only by understanding these keys are we better able to answer the question "Who is responsible?" in regard to suicide.

For centuries the debate has raged about which is more determinative for human behavior, heredity or environment. Unfortunately, the question has generally been raised in just that fashion—as an "or" question rather than an "and" question. It is not a matter of "either/or" but "both/and." Both heredity and environment are determinative for human behavior. The Bible reflects both parts of this equation as it points to our inheritance of sin, calls parents to responsibility, and then cautions against keeping the wrong kind of company or being in the wrong kind of places. But according to the Bible neither our inherited propensity to sin nor our situation in life absolves us of ultimate responsibility for our actions.

As I see it, human motivation is like the four legs of a table. One leg is the factor of heredity, what is passed on to us genetically. The second leg is the biochemical factor. The third is the family factor, and the fourth, the situational factor.

I am proposing that only as we understand the interplay of these four elements will we understand human behavior in general and suicidal behavior in particular. There continue to be those, especially in the medical field, who attribute almost all behavior, normal and abnormal, to genetic or biochemical factors. On the other hand, there are those, usually from the nonmedical helping professions, who want to attribute all behavior to the influence of the family. This latter group has heaped tremendous guilt on families as they have said or implied that whatever goes wrong with children is the fault of poor child-rearing. In other words, the family is to blame. The other side of this coin is that the children have thus been supported in believing they are the hapless victims of inadequate parents.

Few among us today would lay all the blame of bad outcomes at the foot of the fourth element, the situational factors. So convincing have been the proponents of the first three approaches that few informed people would ignore the genetic, biochemical, and family factors in shaping human behavior. Increasing numbers, though, of psychiatrists and therapists of all persuasions recognize the genetic and family factors in shaping human behavior, but ask of the patient/client, "Now what are you going to do about the problem you are facing?" In other words, we can speculate from now until Christ's coming again, and we may not be able to explain the why of our behavior. But answering that question positively is not necessarily a prerequisite for changing our current response to the situation. As the saying among some counselors goes, "Insight cures one thing—ignorance." In other words, insight in and of itself changes nothing. Insight plus positive action is a powerful force for change.

Therefore, if we are to understand human behavior, including suicidal behavior, we have to look at the four-legged stool of human motivation. Only as we consider genetic, biochemical, family, and situational factors will we understand some of the whys of human behavior.

You may be asking, though, is this just a naturalistic explanation of how we humans act? Where is God in all this? The answer, quite simply, is, "He is in all of this." Life is a gift from God and we are his creatures. However, he creates us as free moral agents with the power of choice and the responsibility for the choices we make. He entrusts us to the human, therefore fallen, process through conception, gestation, birth, life, and death. God creates us and he sustains us. His will for us is that we love him and our neighbor, thereby experiencing Jesus' promise, "I came that they may have life, and have it abundantly" (John 10:10, RSV).

Dag Hammarskjøld, the late Secretary General of the United Nations, observed, "The frame of our destiny is not ours to choose. What we put into it is." The frame of our destiny includes the "givens" of our lives—when and to whom and where and into what circumstances we were born. These are the givens of life, but the message of the Gospel is that these reflect both the will of God and the fallen nature into which we are born. Responsibility is not eradicated by these givens, but it is within them that our choices are made. "Given the givens," God calls us toward our full possibilities.

1. The genetic factor

A part of the frame of our destiny is our genetic inheritance. Increasing evidence supports the assertion that our genetic inheritance is a more powerful influence on our lives than many had earlier believed. The research on the major illnesses in recent years gives strong credence to the genetic factor in such areas as heart disease, obesity, cancer, diabetes, and depression.

Humans carry twenty-two pairs of numbered chromosomes, plus a pair that determines sex. One chromosome in each pair is derived from one of the two parents. Chromosomes are bundles of genetic information that form from the nucleus of each cell when cells divide. In recent years several locations within the chromosomes have been identified as sites of specific fragments of genetic information, or genes.

In regard to suicide, a number of researchers have concluded that genes in chromosome six are sometimes linked to depression as well as to multiple sclerosis and a common form of diabetes. Dr. Lowell R. Weitkamp of the University of Rochester, after studying families where depression is common, concludes that "genes at a locus on chromosome six make a major contribution to susceptibility to depressive illness."[1]

Neither this research, which is continuing, nor other research in this field maintains that depression is "caused" by genes. Rather, genes seem to predispose some people to develop depression under certain environmental influences. Also, many researchers in this field claim that the inheritance of depression is much too complex to be explained by a single, isolated gene.

It has been difficult to distinguish between the imitative factor and the genetic factor of suicidal behavior in a family that has a history of a number of suicides. In other words, when several suicides occur in one family over several generations, were they caused as suicide was "modeled" within the family as a way of dealing with problems—or was there a genetic factor? Although suicide does in fact have an enticing effect that at least makes the idea more viable in the minds of certain people, we now know enough to understand that in some families, there is strong suggestion of a genetic predilection to suicide.

In a study reported by M. T. Tsuang in *The Journal of Clinical Psychiatry,* it was found that relatives of psychiatric patients who committed suicide were themselves more likely to have committed suicide than relatives of nonsuicides. Moreover, this was true for relatives of depressed and manic suicides but not for schizophrenic suicides.[2] In another study done by F. Schlusinger and others, the possible role of genetic factors is more clearly seen. This was a Danish study of the adoptive and biologic relatives of 5,483 adoptees. Fifty-seven of the adoptees committed suicide and they were much more likely than a group that matched them in sex, age, and social class to have biologic relatives who committed suicide. None of their adoptive relatives had committed suicide. In this same study, another matched group of nonadoptees were studied. In this group, there were 34 suicides, 23 fewer than among the adoptees.[3] A different study of adoptees found a similar high correlation of suicide in the biologic relatives.[4]

In studies of identical twins, there has also been shown to be genetic factors in suicide. While ten sets of identical twins who have both committed suicide have been reported in medical literature, there has been no report in which both fraternal twins have committed suicide.[5]

Again, all of this information needs to be set in context. If there is suicide in a family, does that mean that the members of that family are helpless in the face of suicide? No. We are products of our past, not prisoners of it. Even in families where there may be a genetic predilection to suicide, there are far more family members who do not commit suicide than there are who do. Again, the words of Dag Hammarskøld are important: "The frame of our destiny is not ours to choose. What we put into it is." Although some have as a part of the "frame of their destiny" a possible genetic inclination toward suicide, the key is their response to that inclination.

2. The biochemical factor

Biochemical factors have been clearly linked to suicide. For instance, many persons who are manic depressives and therefore subject to high and low mood fluctuations are at high risk for suicide. Although there often are contributing other factors in the lives of manic depressive persons, this illness is clearly related to a biochemical imbalance. The best medication found to treat manic depression is lithium carbonate, which is a naturally occurring mineral. If excessive high and low moods can be evened out by a natural mineral, clearly biochemistry plays a role in at least some of the occurrences of suicide.

Added to manic depression, other biochemical imbalances are related to depression and suicide. Among these are premenstrual syndrome, postpartum depression, diabetes, and schizophrenia. In each of these cases, a person's biochemistry can undergo changes which result in depression and therefore distortion of reality that can lead a person toward suicide.

This came home to me recently as I talked with a friend from college days. He recounted days in college when he would feel lifeless and depressed. After a time, this darkness would pass only to return again some weeks later. These mood swings even resulted in the breakup of a serious relationship with a woman he was dating. Only after college and while going through a military physical exam did he discover that he was diabetic and that the mood swings were related to the imbalance of his insulin. One wonders how many persons have taken their lives in the midst of an undiagnosed or untreated diabetic depression.

David Comings, a geneticist at the City of Hope Medical Center in Duarte, California, has found a link between suicide and biochemistry.

Comings discovered that the brains of people who commit suicide often contain abnormal protein also found in the brains of people with multiple sclerosis. Prior to his discovery, multiple sclerosis had already been linked with a class of substances called human leukocyte antigens (HLA), which are essential to the immune system in humans. These substances, which are proteins, are produced by the body's cells, and their production is controlled by a specific group of genes on chromosome six. Though these kinds of studies are providing some hope for improving our understanding of depression and suicide, most of the studies still remain somewhat inconclusive.[6]

Another development in the field of biochemistry holds some promise of unraveling the mystery of suicide and of predicting suicide in some persons. Three groups of investigators have found that lower levels of the transmitters in the brain that are identified as 5-HIAA and 5-HPT are related to suicidal behavior or aggression. These transmitters are a substance called serotonin, the level of which can be detected by a spinal tap. Studies have shown that some persons have a lower level of this cerebral spinal fluid. These studies, done primarily with men, have revealed that among both suicidal and violently aggressive persons, lower than normal levels of serotonin have been found. There is some indication that this low level also relates to less control of impulses. Although there are still factors not fully explained in this

research, it does represent the most compelling evidence of a link
between biochemistry and suicidal behavior.[7]

Given this discussion of biochemistry and suicide, let us look at
a common malady that can contribute to depression, but which
can be treated with drugs.

Susan, a thirty-six-year-old mother of two children, six and
eight, had found herself depressed for several months. She did
not label her feelings as depression. Instead she just sensed she
was going through one of those down times she had experienced for some years.

There were some reasons for being down. She was not feeling
particularly fulfilled as a homemaker, the kids were getting on
her nerves, and her husband was neither sympathetic nor supportive. Another contributing factor to the down time was her
trouble with allergies. Unable to take antihistamines, Susan
seemed to just have to "ride out" the allergy season. In a visit
with her family physician, though, Susan mentioned the allergies. Her physician had just been reading that some allergy suf-
ferers who could not take other medication had gotten relief
from mild anti-depressants. Susan thought facetiously, *Why not
get high and dry at the same time?* The doctor prescribed some
anti-depressants, and Susan quickly began to sense relief from
the allergy symptoms.

She also began to get perspective on her depression. She
began to be more assertive about getting time just to herself.
She confronted her husband about his lack of understanding
and lack of time with her. Susan began seeking some outside
interests including volunteer work in the office of a friend who
was running for city council. It seemed that life had taken on a
different hue almost overnight.

Was Susan's depression due to environmental factors or was
there a chemical imbalance contributing to the depression?
The answer is probably both. But as the chemical imbalance
was dealt with, she was more able to deal with the environmental factors. Susan was the benefactor of the research that continues to go on regarding depression and its treatment.

What does all this research tell us? Should we conclude that we
are mere robots controlled by our body chemistry and therefore
have no responsibility for or even choice in what we decide to do?
Hardly. Remember the analogy of the four-legged table of human

motivation. The biochemical factors are only one leg of this stool, and these researchers do not assert that all the mystery of suicide in particular or human behavior in general is unraveled by their discoveries. They are doing needed and helpful research, however, that enables us to fit more of the pieces of the puzzle together. They are providing help not only in understanding suicide but also in predicting, preventing, and treating it. As Christians, we should take off our hats to such scientists as these.

3. The family factor

Suicide is not a solitary act. Suicide occurs within the context of a culture, a peer group, and a family. To look at the suicidal person as a solitary figure is to fail to understand the suicide or the attempt. Nevertheless, we must be careful on the one hand not to make the family the "scapegoat" in this drama. On the other hand, to ignore the family factor and pretend that the family plays no role in suicide would do a disservice to the quest to understand suicide.

Two of the finest individuals I know are the parents of a young man who took his life. Early in their marriage this couple made their family a high priority, and, in particular, they tried to be good parents. As Christians they sought to make their faith real and powerful to their children. How do you explain the fact that one child took his life, while the other four children manifest no such tendency and are all doing quite well as they establish their own families and launch their careers? There is a mystery here, and as is the case with so many suicides, we see as the apostle Paul did "through a glass darkly."

The mystery manifests itself in the reality that some unhealthy and inadequate parents rear children who seem never to be suicidal while some healthy and dedicated parents rear children who take their lives. Some children come out of what seem to be devastatingly destructive environments, and they go on to build successful lives while others reared in what would seem to be ideal circumstances decide at some point that life is not worth living and kill themselves. How do you account for this? The element of mystery is there but we turn again to the four-legged table analogy. The family is one leg of that table. The reality is that families do not cause suicide, but they can contribute to it. The opposite of the latter is true, too—they can help prevent it.

Following World War II and even more in the 1950s, persons working with psychiatric patients began paying more attention to the interactions between patients and their families. As they did so, they began to see patterns emerging that had not been noticed before or had not been recognized as contributors for good or ill to the patient's condition.

With the influence of Sigmund Freud and the psychoanalytic understanding of emotional disturbance, primary attention had been paid to the individual, his history, and his internal responses. With the advent of what has come to be known as family therapy, consideration has been given to these individual dynamics, but the family of the patient has been given serious consideration as well. In other words, for the family therapist, the family and not just the individual becomes the focus of attention.

What came to be understood by a number of family therapists working somewhat independently was that the family is a system. In other words, the family is an organism that changes, adapts, and continuously influences the behavior of all the members. Now that may seem to be so obvious that to count it a "discovery" is ludicrous, but that understanding has revolutionized the way many professionals are now doing counseling/therapy.

When therapists began asking entire families rather than just the "patient" to come in for an interview, the behavior of the patient often became very understandable in light of his family system. For instance, one of the most common discoveries was the realization that the person who had been identified as the "black sheep," the "causer of all the trouble," was in fact simply the "symptom bearer" of a disturbed family. When attention was given to the family system, it became more clear how each member of the family was "contributing" to the patient's "illness."

John was fourteen when he first tried marijuana. A friend from high school had invited him to "get high" with him. Within a year John was regularly using not only marijuana but also several forms of "uppers," and he was drinking more heavily.

At home things had not been good for some time. His older brother had left home to live with a friend after an argument with his parents. Now John's parents seemed to be bickering constantly and blaming each other for the trouble with their oldest son. Neither parent seemed to pay a lot of attention to John because "he's such a good boy who never gets in trouble."

That attitude changed abruptly when John's mother found a box with marijuana and some pills under John's bed. John was severely interrogated when he got home, and his mother frantically called a friend who was a school counselor. The friend recommended that the parents go with John to see a counselor at the local Family Service Agency. After several visits, things seemed to improve, with John making promises to stop the use of drugs and with his parents, in their concern for him, closer than they had been in months.

Within a few weeks, though, John's parents were back to bickering and all seemed to have returned to "normal." Soon John was back with his old crowd, and he had started drinking again and taking some pills. The story repeated itself, with John's mother discovering the pills, more visits to the counselor, and rather quick improvement. Against the recommendation of the counselor, as soon as things improved, John and his parents dropped out of counseling. Again John's parents seemed to drift apart as soon as the "problem was solved," and eventually John got back on drugs.

Though it was unconscious, John had learned that the way to get his parents to stop arguing and to start being close was for him to get on drugs and let them discover what he was doing. When John's parents had the mutual problem of his drug abuse to deal with, they were close. As soon as that was resolved, they became distant. John, in this family system, had taken on the task of keeping mother and dad together.

Unfortunately, by the next time John got on drugs, the effect on his parents had worn off and rather than seek counseling again, the father became angry and abusive and John's mother became her son's "protector" from his "mean father." Through the same school counselor who had earlier made a referral for the family, John got the help he needed to get off drugs. His parents continued to avoid each other except to argue. John left home for a trade school when he was seventeen. From a family systems perspective, John was the "symptom bearer" of a disturbed family.

If families operate as a system, then it is important to understand some of the implications of that truth. First, every system has subsystems. In the family these would include the parents, the children, and coalitions between members of the family. In the well-functioning family, for instance, the coalition between mother and father would be strong and would withstand unreasonable demands made by the children. In another family, that parental bond may not be strong enough to withstand one of the children making a coalition with one of the parents against the other parent. For example, the father tells the teenage daughter she cannot go to a local youth hangout by herself on Friday night. The daughter goes to the mother, pleads her case, and because both mother and daughter "know" that the father can be "unreasonable" and "out of it," they conspire to let the daughter have her way and not let father know. Thus, the parental bond is weak and does not withstand the daughter's assault.

Within a family, subsystems change according to the situation, and coalitions may be made, for instance, between father and son over against mother and daughter about such a trivial item as selections on television. But to understand families, the various subsystems need to be examined.

Another implication of the family as a system is the realization that each family has its own ways of maintaining equilibrium. When disruptions occur in the family such as illness, death, or economic change, the system will be changed accordingly. Compensations are made so that in the case of the death of the father, often the eldest son "takes dad's place in the family" and begins to fulfill the father role.

One of the ways families have of maintaining equilibrium is by responding to the feedback they receive. If mother and the oldest daughter begin arguing and the younger daughter becomes scared and starts crying, mother and daughter stop arguing and pay attention to little sister. Thus, little sister gets the "message" that when mother and sister argue, the way to get them to stop is to start crying. The "message" of this feedback to mother and older sister is that a way to keep the argument from getting too bad is to fight in front of little sister and she'll stop the fighting. This is all "unconscious," but it is no less an important part of the feedback system of this family.

The concept of boundaries is another vital part of the understanding of the family as a system. Family boundaries distinguish the family from its environment and also divide family subsystems. These boundaries need to be strong enough to maintain the identity and integrity of the unit and yet flexible enough to permit interaction with the outside world and across boundaries within the family. According to some studies of dysfunctional families, the family boundary becomes so rigid that the family shuts itself off from the rest of the world. This promotes paranoia, makes it extremely difficult to leave the family, and can lead to the self-destruction of the family.

Within the family, boundaries may become confused as a child becomes "parentfied" and starts functioning as if he were a parent rather than a child. This occurs sometimes in the case of the "helpless parent" who lets "little mother" or the "little man" take over. Also, the boundary of a subsystem may become rigid and a coalition between a parent and a child may close off interaction with the rest of the family. For example, a mother becomes immobilized by depression and is hospitalized. In the interim, the sixteen-year-old daughter takes over the role of mother in the house and gets very close to her father. When mother comes home, the daughter does not easily relinquish her newfound role. Mother may then conclude, "I'm not needed around here anymore."

In family systems roles are important. The role we are assigned in the family depends on such factors as birth order, sex, energy level, intelligence, athletic ability, social skills, appearance, and what is happening in the family at our birth. Families assign such labels as "black sheep," "stupid," "beautiful," "sensitive," "athlete," "tomboy," "charmer," "savior," "helpless," and "sickly." Sometimes the role is reflected in the name chosen. Being named Thomas for a wealthy uncle conveys a very different message from being named Thomas for an alcoholic grandfather who killed himself. In any event, in the healthiest families there is considerable role flexibility.

The place of the family in the family life cycle determines how the family system will work at that time. A family at the stage of childbearing will operate very differently from a family with older youth at the child-launching stage. A family gets in trouble when it gets "stuck" in one stage of the family life cycle. For instance, it is not uncommon to see one or both parents who are in a bad marriage desperately attempt to keep the last child from leaving home. This may be out of fear that when that child leaves, the marriage will fall apart. Or it may be the fear that when active child-rearing ends, life will lose its meaning.

Finally, as was alluded to earlier, there is the phenomenon of the "identified patient" in the family. This is usually a child but can be one of the parents. This person is the disturber, the rebel, the delinquent, or the "sick" member of the family. The behavior of this person drives the family to seek professional help to "fix" him or her. Therefore, this person is the identified patient and is deemed to be the only one in the family who needs help. A wise therapist will not buy this diagnosis and invites the entire family in for a consultation or therapy. What is discovered is that the identified patient is a symptom of a larger problem within the family to which all members are contributing in varying degrees. Even the "good" child who never rocks the boat is contributing, albeit unconsciously, to the disturbance in the family.

What does all this explanation of the family system have to do with suicide? It is a reminder to us that suicide occurs within the context of a family. Suicide is not a solitary act. Suicide involves the family, and the family is intertwined in the suicide process in ways that are subtle and obvious, profound and simple. Finally, this understanding of the family as a system tells us that for the suicidal person to be helped significantly, the family probably needs help, too.

Does admitting that the family, not just the suicidal person, needs help imply the family is "at fault"? It implies that one member of the system is about to exit the system by suicide. If he is to be stopped, attention needs to be given to that system and how, even unconsciously, it is contributing to the suicide crisis. "Blame" and "fault" are not the issues. The issue is, "Will this family face the pain of confronting what is going on within it so that they can prevent a suicide and learn to function better?"

Where does the family get the help required? If the suicidal member is in counseling or hospitalized, then surely the therapeutic team will involve the family in the process. This may be only a few sessions with individual members, but it could be a series of sessions with the whole family present with the therapist.

If you do not already have such access to someone who does family therapy, talk to several counselors in your area to discover more about the availability of family therapy. You can write the American Association of Marriage and Family Therapy (924 W. Ninth Street, Upland, CA 91786). This association will send you a list of trained family therapists in your area. Also, you can check with a school counselor for a referral or the name of a family service agency.

Family therapy is demanding, sometimes frightening, but also powerful. Part of its power is the insight that can be fairly quickly gained into what is happening within the family. Notice the insight gained from a brief part of one family therapy session conducted three weeks after the father had nearly killed himself by a drug overdose:

One of the children said in response to a routine question, "Well, we all fought with Dad about a lot of things until about three weeks ago."
Therapist: "What happened then?"
Child: "I don't know. We just all quit. Maybe we got tired of it, always fighting with him."
Therapist: "You think you gave up on him?"
Child: "Maybe."
Therapist to the father: "So maybe the family gave up on you, and you sensed it. And you then gave up on yourself and took the pills."
The father: "Maybe I did. I had never thought of it that way."[8]

In a few brief moments, insight is gained into what may have silently triggered this suicide attempt.

Remember, this emphasis on the family does not imply that the family "causes" the suicidal person to be suicidal. But the family may be one part of the problem and therefore can be one part of the solution.

4. The situational factor

When parents feel especially guilty if their child "goes wrong" or has problems, often the parents are being over-responsible for the behavior of that child. There is a denial of the power of the situational factors present in every life. There are limits to what a parent can do to insure his children's success or happiness. The parent has a few short years when the child is his total charge. Within five or six years the child spends six to eight hours a day in school. From an early age most children are exposed to the wider world through television. As the teenage years approach, the peer group becomes increasingly powerful in the young person's life.

In late adolescence, most young people move even farther from parental influence as they leave home for school, jobs, or military service.

Does this deny the responsibility of parents in rearing emotionally healthy, well-functioning children? No. It simply sets the responsibility of parents in the context of the limits of their powers over against other outside influences that shape the child's life. A well-reared child may face situations that virtually overwhelm his coping abilities. In such situations, when the pain becomes so intense, some of these well-reared children attempt or complete suicide.

What are some of the situations that ensnare persons to the extent that suicide seems the only way out? For some, addiction to or abuse of alcohol and other drugs is the road that leads to suicide. Increasingly available are drugs of all types and of varying lethality. For many persons who escape through drugs, to "slip out of life quietly" with an overdose becomes powerfully seductive.

Some persons, given a tendency toward violence, begin to associate with other death-darers. A culture of violence emerges and the agenda for life becomes the thrill of fondling forms of violence. Motorcycle clubs, racing clubs, and other groups that thrive on danger can encourage some toward subintentioned deaths.

Financial failure exacts its toll, and it seems especially to come at a demanding price for men. Many men and some women hang all their self-worth on the peg of succeeding in their work. When that one source of self-worth crumbles, life can seem useless. Witness the rise of suicide during times of economic stress, and the number of retired men who take their lives.

Divorce can be the most emotionally devastating experience of one's life. Self-worth, emotional and economic security, and social life can be drastically changed when a marriage ends.

The social/political climate can contribute to stress leading to suicide. The "body count" is still continuing with the casualties of the late 1960s young adult generation when all structures of authority were questioned, drugs and sex in many forms were suddenly "okay," and the nation was fighting a divisive war. The heroes were antiheroes and the culture became haunted by death.

For some, the world was turned upside down and the death-force seemed to be winning more battles than the life-force.

Other situational factors could surely be mentioned, but suffice it to say that these kinds of factors play a powerful role in the drama of suicide. Virtually all the enduring strength of a person can be drained given the stress of some situations. When the number four leg of that four-legged stool fails, unless a tricky balancing act is done, the whole thing can fall.

The Limits of Your Responsibility

A friend of mine, serving on the staff of a counseling center where we later worked together, was seeing a city policeman in his mid-thirties in individual counseling. The problem for which the policeman was seeking help was depression with some suicidal thoughts. After a number of weeks of counseling, the policeman decided to terminate the sessions, against the counselor's advice. Several weeks later on a Saturday afternoon, the police officer used his revolver to kill himself.

My friend, seeking some comfort and some perspective, called his professor of counseling. This professor pioneered in the field of pastoral counseling and psychology of religion and had faced suicide in the family in which he grew up. After hearing the story of what had happened, the professor remarked, "Michael, just remember, every tub's gotta sit on its own bottom." This is an unvarnished way of saying that in the final analysis every person is responsible for his/her own actions. The ultimate responsibility rests with the individual. However limited, responsibility is still there with the suicidal person.

Does this mean that you have no responsibility to the person considering suicide? Of course not. But it does mean that you do not carry the total responsibility for what happens to the individual. There are limits to your responsibility.

Given the nature of the Christian faith and, in fact, moral thought in the western tradition, you have a responsibility to care for, comfort, support, confront, and in other ways seek to prevent the death of a suicidal person. From the Christian perspective, life is understood as a gift from God. Each person is to be valued as one of God's creatures created in his image, and each is to be loved.

These two sentences include a multitude of presuppositions about the nature of life, and the implications are manifold. They embody some of the most basic teachings of the Judeo-Christian heritage. For me, they are part of the givens of my existence.

But what are the implications in regard to suicide? First, that you value life and seek to prevent its destruction. Second, that the valuing and cherishing of life is not simply because God commanded it, but because the individual as an individual is important. The teachings and actions of Jesus drive this point home again and again in the gospel narratives. He valued everyone including, to use Mohandas Gandhi's words, "the least, the lost, and the last." Because of this Judeo-Christian heritage, in western society when an individual climbs atop a building or a bridge with the intent to take his life, herculean efforts are made to prevent his death. Even though before he climbed out on that ledge or that steel span, he was an unknown to those who seek his rescue, he has become important to them. Why? Not because of status or position, or wealth. He is important because he is a person! He is a person of worth not by virtue of place or merit, but by virtue of simply being a person!

The third implication of what I have earlier asserted is that we are to love the individual, and that love takes the form of preventing a suicidal person from taking his life. In some circles there is considerable debate about whether preventing a suicide is always a loving act. As I pointed out in the preface of this book, I have not dealt here with the ethical issues surrounding suicide. There are legitimate and compelling ethical issues that need to be discussed. My assumption in this book, however, is that we are talking about preventing suicides where there is reasonable hope for a meaningful existence. Given that assumption, prevention of suicide is a loving act.

In theological and philosophical circles there is even debate about the meaning of love. Those debates are more understandable when we see how central the concept of love is to any moral code. The American theologian who has given the most careful attention to the meaning of love in a Christian context is the late Daniel Day Williams. His core definition of love is "communion in freedom." Now at first glance that hardly seems profound. But into this definition Williams packed the understanding that love is relationship (communion) and that if it is true love, the freedom of the lover and the beloved is maintained. In other words, love is persuasive and not coercive. Therefore, love can be accepted or it can be freely rejected.

This understanding of love has profound implications in suicide prevention. You can offer assistance, support, and many other forms of aid to a suicidal person. But finally it is his to choose whether he will accept the offer. You seek to build relationship—communion—and thereby be one more roadblock on the way that leads to suicide. But not only can the offers of help be rejected, so can the relationship.

The limits of your responsibility are drawn by the freedom of the other person.

Does this mean you never override the wishes of the other person? Does it mean that you so respect his freedom and autonomy that you never use coercion, manipulation, or physical force to prevent suicide? I cannot go this far. I will and have used coercion, manipulation, and physical force to prevent suicide. Why? Because I am aware of the nature of suicide. First, almost all suicidal persons are ambivalent about dying. They may tell you, "Please don't hospitalize me," when that is actually just what they want you to do. They may beg you not to tell the one person who might have the greatest chance of preventing their suicide, and in fact they desperately want you to tell that person. If a person is totally committed to taking his life, he will. Therefore, to take extreme measures to prevent a suicide will work finally only if he is in fact ambivalent. If he is not, and he later does take his life, you can have some comfort in the fact that you did what you could to prevent his death.

The second reason why I would use and have used such drastic measures is the recognition of the faulty reasoning that is characteristic of most suicidal persons. Suicide is not the answer to their problems and it closes off all other options. As we noted in the first chapter, people attempt and complete suicide for a variety of reasons, but the reasons are not reasonable. Why is this? Because the suicidal person has lost perspective. He cannot see another way to deal with his problems. Only when given time and therapy and support will he come to see that suicide would have been a tragic mistake. Why do I believe this? Because I have talked with and read about many people alive today, including some of the most creative people in our society, who at one point thought about or attempted suicide and who now are eternally grateful they did not destroy themselves. Another day brought another view. Therefore, I am willing, within limits, to override another person's freedom temporarily to give him more time and to get him more help.

Does this view violate the view of love I have espoused? No, because I continue to respect the freedom of the other. And ultimately I will not, because I cannot, prevent his death if he is totally, without ambivalence, committed to taking his life.

On a late fall day I stood on a street corner in downtown Dallas and talked with a friend following our racquetball game. He was contemplating suicide. He was in counseling and because the danger of suicide was not imminent, his counselor had chosen not to hospitalize my friend, though she did hospitalize him long enough for a thorough physical. As we talked, I checked out the intensity, frequency, and specificity of his suicidal thoughts. Judging him not to be immediately in danger, I told him once again of my concern for him, and I shared with him some of the gifts I saw in him and what that could mean for the future. He talked with tears in his eyes of the struggle of recent years. He asked me not to worry about him. I told him I was too much of a "mother" not to worry and that not only did I keep checking on him and seeking to be of help because I cared for him, but I also knew how much it would hurt me if he took his life.

We parted and I headed down the street to catch the bus, knowing that at some time and some place my friend could end his life. Would it have been in part my responsibility? Only in the sense that there may have been some things left undone to help him. I have cared, I have called, I have invited him into my home, I have helped develop a network of supportive friends, I have sought work for him, I have let him know of my love. But I am forced back to the reality that the decision is finally his. He carries the ultimate responsibility, not I. But if he takes his life, that only lessens the guilt, not the sadness.

There comes a time in a relationship with a suicidal person for "letting go" without leaving. This is the same process a parent experiences as he gradually relinquishes a child to a wider world and to loyalties to others. The parent lets go, but in the letting go does not leave or abandon the child. So with a suicidal person, whether child or mate or friend, we love and show that love, but we relinquish control because we cannot, finally, control his life.

Is this a denial of all that we have said in this book about suicide prevention? No. It is a realization of the limits of our responsibility. It is not giving up the attempt to prevent suicide. Instead it is testimony to the reality that every person finally and ultimately walks his own road. We cannot walk it for him, for we have our own road to travel. We can help, we can point out the dangers, we can bind up wounds when a stumbling block causes a fall. But the limits of our ability to help are drawn by the other's willingness to accept that help.

In no way should this "letting go" be conveyed as giving up or abandonment. It is not that. Rather it says, "I will help, and I will stand by you, but ultimately you are responsible for you."

Conclusion

Who is responsible? Can all the responsibility be placed at the feet of the genetic factors? Are the biochemical factors responsible? Is the family "at fault"? What about situational factors?

The responsibility for suicide must finally be placed at the feet of the suicidal person. To do otherwise would be to deny the freedom of the individual. But does the individual act alone, and is he all-powerful to resist all the forces leading to suicide? No. Suicide and suicide attempts must be seen in the context of many contributing factors. A simple cause-and-effect explanation must be avoided. Every suicide and every suicide attempt speaks to us of the mystery and the complexity of life.

Because we are human beings who care, we bear the burden of responsibility. But there are limits to our responsibility.

7

Helping a Suicidal Adolescent

She has called you to say she wants to talk with you, she needs to talk to you very soon, and she says it is serious. You set up a time for her to come by the church right after school. This sixteen-year-old junior tells you that she has been thinking about taking her life. You and two of her girlfriends are the only ones who know, and she does not want you to tell her parents or the pastor.

Two youth hang around one night after Bible study to talk with you about a friend, a freshman who moved to town last year. He has never really fit in at school or in the youth group. His humor is inappropriate, and he tries so hard to be "in" that he turns the other kids off. Usually loud and boisterous, he has become quiet and withdrawn. He has talked about suicide before, but in a joking way.

With another youth, you have sensed the disappointment and pain he is feeling. First, a summer accident kept him from playing

---

In many ways, this chapter summarizes the book, reemphasizing some of the points made earlier, as it zeroes in on working with suicide-prone youth. This chapter appeared as "Ministry in a Suicidal Crisis" in *Ministry with Youth in Crisis,* compiled by Richard Ross and Judi Hayes (Nashville: Convention Press, 1988). All rights reserved. Used by permission.

football his junior year. Now the girl he has gone with for a year has broken up with him. He has talked with you a couple of times. Somehow some of the things he has said have left you with a feeling that things are getting serious. You are trying to find a way to discover if he is thinking about suicide.

With these three situations we are well into some of the questions and the fears of dealing with suicidal youth.

Why do young people become suicidal?

That question is asked almost incredulously by most adults. The standard reaction to youth suicide is, "Why suicide when he had his whole life ahead of him?" But to the suicidal young person, what looks like such a prize to adults can look like a long, dark tunnel with neither light nor ending.

The major reason persons of all ages take their lives is to escape from intolerable pain. Other motivations include:

- to punish the survivors.
- to gain attention.
- to manipulate others.
- to join a deceased loved one.
- to avoid punishment.
- to be punished.
- to avoid becoming a "burden."
- to avoid the effects of a dread disease.
- to pursue an irrational, impulsive whim.
- to seek martyrdom.
- to express love.

Another perspective on motivations for suicide draws from the pioneering work done by the psychiatrist Karl Menninger. His proposals regarding the unconscious motivations of suicide were later subdivided by J. A. M. Meerloo in his book *Suicide and Mass Suicide*. Meerloo listed the following as the inferred meaning of the final act of suicidal persons:

- suicide as being killed.
- suicide as killing.
- suicide as communicating.
- suicide as getting revenge.
- suicide as escape.
- suicide as magic reversal or transformation.[1]

Of course, most suicides are a result of a mixture of these motives; and we are always imprecise in understanding fully the motives because the death has taken away our opportunity to look in the eyes of the person and ask, "Why?"

But looking at these general classifications for suicidal behavior still does not answer fully the question we asked above. We must look at contributing factors.

What are the contributing factors to youth suicide?

The first contributing factor is the nature of adolescence itself.—In the fifties, Remmers and Radler in their book, *The American Teenager,* described the predicament of the adolescent as a person whose energies are already sapped by the sheer process of physical growth; caught up in a whirl of school work and social activities in and out of school; confronted by decisions that will affect his entire life; confused by the shifting attitudes of parents, teachers, and society in general, all of whom doubt him and his behavior; bewildered by the complex and rapidly changing civilization into which he must soon fit, assuming all the responsibilities of maturity.[2]

Youth workers, of course, know firsthand the complexities and confusions of adolescence because of the youth with whom they work week by week. They can experience some of the fright an adolescent feels in this time. But we must realize that many adults can't or won't begin to fathom how it feels to be a teenager. Studies have shown the willingness of parents of adolescents to reminisce about their days in junior high or high school. But when those parents are asked to remember the feelings of those days, they balk. Apparently, we want to reminisce nostalgically; but we don't want to recall the embarrassing moments, the awkwardness, the fear of rejection, the hurt, the loneliness.

The changing moral climate of our nation contributes to youth suicide.—Adolescents need firm moral guidelines. They are changing so quickly physically, emotionally, and socially that they need stability and firmness in as much of the world around them as possible. What remains solid and dependable for young persons in the potentially difficult years of adolescence? One source of support is a society where the moral guidelines are firm. But what happens if the rules of society keep changing and the morals are objects of debate rather than reliable guideposts? Then a primary source of support has become a shaky foundation.

The family is often a contributing factor in youth suicide. —A warning is needed here. Too often and sometimes automatically, the family has been pegged the culprit in youth suicide. This issue is much too complex to be that simplistic. Young people who have grown up in good, healthy families take their lives. Inevitably the family feels guilty and assumes that they surely could have done something to prevent this death, but the family is just one factor in a suicide. Some persons have a biochemical proclivity toward depression and suicide. Also, given the right combination of blows to the ego and the impulsiveness of youth, suicide occurs even among "healthy" young people. Having said that, we must also say that family factors such as the lack of or poor communication, divorce, physical and sexual abuse, mobility, and pressure to succeed do contribute to youth suicide.

Another contributing factor to youth suicide is alcohol or other drugs. —A study of youth suicide in Dallas County done by the Dallas Suicide and Crisis Center indicated that alcohol consumption and the easy availability of handguns were two of the most significant factors in teenage suicide.

More than one half of all suicides in the nation are linked to alcohol. Among young people who take their lives or attempt to do so are habitual alcohol abusers, some who get drunk to "get up their courage" to take their lives, and youth who drink alcohol and then knowingly take drugs that are lethal when combined with alcohol.

Lethal, illegal drugs other than alcohol are frequently used to commit suicide, but many of these deaths are labeled "accidental." Prescription drugs in the family medicine cabinet are, of course, the means of many attempts and many "successful" suicides of young people.

The easy availability of a means to kill oneself is also a factor. — These means include guns, cars, and drugs. In one year, 62 percent of all suicides in America among the age group fifteen to twenty-four used guns.[3]

A factor that must be considered is the overall level of violence in our society and the glorification of much of that violence. —A level of homicides is accepted in the United States as normal that would be a disgrace to most western and many third-world nations. Violent means of handling problems are regularly and graphically portrayed on television and in movies. American youth live in a violent world. During the last twenty years or so, the overall national mortality rate has declined; but among fifteen- to twenty-four-year-olds, suicides have increased 136 percent and homicides have increased 164 percent.[4]

A romantic view of death among teens is a factor. —Most youth have a sense of immortality. They walk in the street daring cars to hit them. They drive fast and recklessly with little sense of how fragile life actually is or how quickly it can end.

For the average adolescent death is mysterious but not always real because it seems so remote. One youth who later took his life said, "Death doesn't mean one is never to be seen again."[5] That was written by a teenager who took his life.

Even the death of a friend, even a death by suicide, may not break this romantic view of death. The attention and love poured out for a teenager who has died can entice some young persons to seek that same attention and love by suicide.

Mental illness must be included as one of the factors to consider. —The two forms of mental illness most frequently seen in youth suicide are depression and schizophrenia. Although all suicidal persons are in need of help and counseling, not all would be clinically diagnosed as mentally ill.

Later we will look more closely at adolescent depression. Schizophrenia, on the other hand, is a mental illness that generally manifests itself first in late adolescence or young adulthood. In spite of the common misconceptions, it is not the phenomenon of dual or multiple personalities. The manifestation one might see as a youth minister is that the youth has broken with reality and is seeing things, imagining things, and hearing things that are unreal. Suicide attempts are often made in the early stages of this illness.[6]

Suicide itself is a factor in youth suicide. —Suicide begets suicide. When a teenager or a role model or certainly a parent takes his or her life, it implants strongly the idea among those affected that suicide is an option when dealing with life's problems.

Other contributing factors include such things as radical "futurelessness" and "Autoerotic" deaths. —In a seminar dealing with war and peace, Robert J. Lifton, then on the faculty of Yale University, reported the factor of what psychologists call a "radical sense of futurelessness" as an element in youth suicide. This is the sense on the part of the young person that nuclear destruction is so certain that it does not matter if one kills himself because we will all be killed eventually in a nuclear holocaust.[7]

Although a small minority of deaths by suicide, "autoerotic" deaths have shown up in recent years in larger numbers. These deaths, in fact, are accidental or seem to be. Approximately 500 to 1,000 occur in America each year, and most of those are adolescent boys. These deaths occur as the adolescent simultaneously masturbates and achieves near asphyxiation, usually induced by a noose around the neck. This supposedly heightens sexual pleasure, but many lose consciousness and die.[8]

Rock music is often associated with youth suicide. Some lyrics and styles of rock music paint an alluring picture of death. Some rock groups seem to be death oriented. Many are even blatantly satanic. Although rock music may be a factor in some adolescent suicides, the distorted perspective and downward spiral of the adolescent draws him or her toward the sickness in some rock music. To say rock music caused a youth suicide is too simplistic. It may have been a contributing factor, but all the blame cannot be put at the feet of rock music.

The fantasy game "Dungeons and Dragons" and other such games have been linked in the media to youth suicide. Some young persons who were avid D & D players have committed suicide. But did D & D cause the suicides? As a parent and as a pastor, I am opposed to my children or members of my youth group getting involved in D & D because of the occult images and because of the violence of the role-playing. I believe these kinds of games attract some youth with significant problems. It has yet to be shown, however, that these fantasy games are a direct link to suicide. I do believe that some young people who are in the suicidal process are attracted to such games.

Finally, in recent years the worship of Satan by youth cults has been linked to suicides. When youth become disturbed enough to turn to Satan, their world is turning upside down; and mutilation, murder, and suicide can become the symbols of one's commitment.

Many more factors could be listed, but we turn now to dealing with the actual crisis.

How can one recognize the crisis?

What signs might indicate that a young person is considering taking his/her life?—The major warning signs of adolescent suicide include:

• a sudden change in behavior, such as amount of talking or daring or violent behavior, changes in friends, eating, sleeping, or appearance.

• a recent traumatic event, such as the death of a friend or a family member, parents' divorce, failure in school, serious physical illness, or the breakup of a romance.

• withdrawal, including quietness and dropping out of normal activities.

• preoccupation about death and related themes.

• threatening or talking about suicide, including leaving suicide notes.

• giving away prized possessions.

• seeming to say good-bye to friends.

• getting in trouble with law enforcement when this has not happened in the past.

• abusing drugs and alcohol, especially if this has not been done before.

• reporting chronic trouble at home.

• living away from home, especially if it was because of trouble with parents.

• having recently moved to a new community but not yet feeling a part of a new group.

• getting or inquiring about a means to attempt suicide.

• pronounced inability to communicate or refusal to talk about what is wrong.

• dropping out of counseling.

• marked and unusual disorganization.

• frequently "messing up" in a way that seems almost deliberate.

• a series of successes that have added a lot of pressure.

• prolonged boredom, particularly if it is because of a lack of extracurricular activities or a lack of direction, interests, or goals.

• numerous physical complaints, such as headaches, stomach aches, etc.

• expressing feelings of helplessness and hopelessness.

- irrational ideas, especially if they are associated with voices or other forms of delusion.
- rapid weight gain or loss.
- general increase in self-destructive behavior, such as driving fast, using drugs and alcohol, or violence and belligerence.

This list may look a bit overwhelming, and you may be able to identify some young people who have shown some of these signs. The important thing to remember, though, is that you are looking for a series of signs that spell at the least the possibility of a looming suicidal crisis. You obviously should not jump to the conclusion that a young person is suicidal just because one of the above signs appears.

But if you were to look back over that list and mention one overriding factor that seemed to characterize all of them, what would it be? I would suggest "unexplained change." Something has changed, and you don't know why. I hope that one of the results of your reading and rereading this chapter is that you will become so sensitive to unexplained change among your young people that you cannot ignore it.

Anyone who has worked in suicide prevention for long will tell you that you begin to develop an instinct that becomes an early warning signal. Slowly or all of a sudden, you begin to put the pieces of the puzzle together in your mind; and you say to yourself, "I don't know what's happening, but I need to find out." You are learning to listen to the language of behavior. This is one of the most crucial skills in suicide prevention, especially with youth.

What are the verbal clues?—We must also listen to the verbal clues a youth may use to signal his intent about suicide. Those clues may include some of these:

"Do you think someone can come back after she's dead?"
"They're going to be sorry."
"I've had it. Life isn't worth it."
"I can't go on without him."
"Living is stupid. It's a hassle."
"You've meant a lot to me. You helped. Thanks."
"Nobody understands me. I don't think they ever will."
"I'm thinking about killing myself."
"How do you will your body to a medical school?"
"I think they'd rather see me dead than doing drugs."

"If I'm pregnant, I'm going to kill myself."
"I'm through. It's not worth the hassle."
"See you on the other side."
"It all looks dark. All I see is darkness."
"Maybe they'll care after I'm dead."
"You won't have to worry about me being a problem anymore."
"Do you know if a whole bottle of aspirin can kill you?"
"Do you know where I can get a gun?"
"I'm a failure. I'll never be what I thought I could be."
Some of these verbal clues are fairly obvious. Others might be ignored unless you are really listening.

How do you spot adolescent depression?—Of course, many of the signs mentioned above are signs of adolescent depression, but depression deserves special attention because whatever the causes of a particular suicide attempt, depression is going to be the emotion present in almost all adolescent attempts.

According to psychiatrist Hugh Storrow, professor of psychiatry at the University of Kentucky College of Medicine, "Depression is exaggerated sadness coupled with pessimism, and pessimism is the essential component that distinguishes depression from the ordinary 'low' feelings that we all experience from time to time. The depressed person is not simply sad; he has the impression that his sadness will persist indefinitely regardless of what he does about it."[9]

In light of Storrow's words, note this interesting response made by Pamela Cantor, an expert in adolescent suicide and past president of the American Association of Suicidology, when she was asked why youth who take their lives feel so hopeless: "They suffer from a kind of tunnel vision. They are looking down a long, dark tunnel, and all they see is darkness. They don't know that there is light outside and at the end of the tunnel. They don't know where in the tunnel they are; they think it goes on forever."[10]

But what are the recognizable signs of depression in adolescents? While adolescents sixteen or over may have the same symptoms as adults, younger adolescents often will not present the same symptoms. That is one reason adolescent depression often goes undetected.

Frank B. Minirth and Paul D. Meier, Christian psychiatrists who have specialized in the treatment of depression, observe:

"When adults become depressed they look depressed and act depressed. However, when adolescents become depressed, their depression is presented in a somewhat atypical manner. Instead of looking and acting depressed, they may act out their depression. Very moral, conscientious teen-agers may begin to steal, to lie, to take illegal drugs, or to misbehave sexually as a result of being depressed emotionally."[11]

These experts return us to that issue of "unexplained change." When it is present, we should begin questioning what is going on. In other words, when in doubt, check it out.

But you may be asking: "What do I do if I check it out and my suspicions are correct? What steps can I take to really help this young person?" That is the focus of the last part of this chapter.

What steps can one take with a suicidal youth?

You have become aware of this potential crisis (1) by listening to the language of behavior and/or verbal clues, (2) indirectly when a friend or parent has talked to you, or (3) because the individual has sought you out. You have determined that you should talk to the person. How do you do it?

Build from your position of strength. —Realize that you will be helping this young person from your position of strength. Recognize and remember that strength as you seek to be used of God to help a troubled youth.

Your position of strength is made up of at least these components:

- your relationship to the Lord.
- your relationship with the youth.
- your relationship with the youth's family.
- your relationship with the youth's friends.
- the availability through the church and other means of creating a support group for the youth.

In talking with the youth, you want to move from strength to strength. By that I mean, you need to be conscious of the strengths you have to work with lest you feel overwhelmed and come across as if you and the situation are hopeless. You want to recognize and stress the strengths of the youth. Almost all suicidal people have ambivalent feelings about living and dying. A part of them wants to live, and a part of them wants to die. Draw on that part of them that wants to live and the strengths they have exhibited to do that.

Talk with the youth. —Let's assume that the young person visits you in your office. Either you took the initiative to ask him to come by, or he asked to talk to you. How do you begin?

First, begin by exploring what is happening in the youth's life. Whether he is open and free or more reticent about reporting what's happening, listen carefully. With the youth whom you asked to come by your office, you may begin by mentioning some of the things you've noticed that have raised concerns in your own mind; or you may mention the concerns that have been expressed to you by the youth's friends.

Do not mention suicide. You are merely exploring with special attention how what is happening is being interpreted by the youth. Remember that things which may seem trivial or silly to you as an adult can be of monumental importance to that youth. Do not trivialize or ridicule something that seems deserving of both but to the young person is important and even devastating.

One fifteen-year-old girl who had attempted suicide said: "We don't have a right to have problems. Parents only remember the good times." Are you that kind of parent? Teenagers need someone to listen to them about problems whether they seem serious or unimportant.

In the midst of this initial exploration, keep asking yourself questions like:

"Who are her heroes/models, and what does that tell me?"

"What are his dreams?"

"What is essential for her self-worth?"

"Who are those people who are special to her?"

"What is it like to live in his family?"

At this point you should have a pretty good reading on whether suicide is being considered.

Second, raise the question of suicide. The obvious question here is, "Will mentioning it just give the person the idea?" First, most of today's adolescents who are in significant pain or difficulty have already thought about it. Second, the chance is remote that your mentioning it would provide the idea. Third, what is the alternative? Just hoping it isn't so?

You raise the question by saying something like this: "Are you so down that you've thought about hurting yourself?" Or you may go with a more general question like, "What ways out of this situation have you considered?" I would suggest at this point that you avoid specifically asking about suicide lest the youth recoil and deny it. But you need to keep asking enough to discover if suicide has been or is being considered as an option.

Third, determine the level of danger. At this point, you are at a crossroads. Either the youth is suicidal or not; and if suicidal, he is either in immediate danger or he is not,

If the youth says he has not been contemplating suicide and you believe that, help him to identify the issues being faced and then explore and identify ways to deal with those issues. Help the young person see ways to get the support needed. That may include periodic visits with you, formal counseling with a Christian counselor, a different kind of involvement with a youth group, getting into a prayer and share or Bible study group, or many other options. You may also seek the youth's permission to tell a few other key people about what is happening so that they can be in prayer and also be more involved in this youth's life. Keep monitoring this situation lest what was not a suicidal crisis becomes one.

But what if the answer is positive to your implied question about suicide? Determine the danger of the situation by asking a series of questions:

"How long have you been thinking about taking your life?"

"Have you thought about how you would do it?"

"Do you have the pills/gun/rope/razor/etc.?"

"Have you attempted suicide before?"

"Has anyone in your family ever taken his life?"

"Have you made arrangements for your death?"

"Are you drinking or using any other drugs?"

Things get scary at this point because we are dealing with life and death. And it may seem to you that you are in way over your head. Realize that you are not going to be a Lone Ranger suicide preventer. You are on the frontline of defense against suicide, but you are going to call troops in to help in this battle.

If the youth has answered some of these questions positively, then you do have a serious situation with real potential for danger. If the youth has a definite plan and an available and lethal method, he is serious about suicide. If this is combined with previous attempts, a family history of suicide, and/or the use of alcohol/drugs, you've got a full-blown suicidal crisis.

Scared? That's understandable. Let God use that fear to help you be at your best in this situation. To the youth involved you need to appear as calm and confident as possible.

Whether the youth has given you indications that this is a dangerous and immediate crisis or that he has "just" been thinking about suicide with no further plans toward it, these guidelines will help you in your conversation with the young person.

1. Pray throughout this experience. Pray especially for wisdom and discernment and the guidance of the Holy Spirit. Pray for strength because this crisis can become draining.

2. Listen carefully while continuing to point out that death is irreversible. Listen to the words that are spoken, but seek the meaning behind them. Listen also to the language of behavior. All this time, the hard reality of death needs to be asserted. As has been pointed out before, suicide is a very permanent solution to a temporary problem.

Most adolescents have a romantic view of death. In a sense they feel they are invulnerable to it. But even through the death of a family member or a friend, conceptually youth have a hard time conceiving that death is really the end of life on earth.

3. Listen for and reinforce those persons and things that still give the youth hope and joy. Almost all suicidal persons are ambivalent about suicide. Draw on and emphasize those persons and things that keep this teenager going.

Be careful about trying to shame the youth about what his suicide would do to family members and friends. You can point out the pain it will cause, but don't relay on shame to cause a change of mind. Remember that for some suicidal persons, pain is what they want to inflict on others by their death.

4. Remain hopeful without dismissing the seriousness of the situation. Communicate hope and confidence that things can be turned for the better. Do this without being flippant.

Aaron Beck of the University of Pennsylvania School of Medicine is a preeminent authority on depression and suicide. He says that hopelessness in the depressed person is a primary sign of the danger of suicide. In this conversation you need to counter despair with hope.

5. Do not be misled by easy assurances that everything is now OK. If the young person seems genuinely depressed and has indicated some suicidal thoughts, do not let him get away by telling

you how much you have helped and how much better he feels after having talked with you. That feeds your ego; but some suicidal young people have done this, left the counselor, and killed themselves.

Almost all suicidal persons have gone through a long process to get to the point of suicide, and they will not come out of it quickly. In fact, a dangerous time is when they start getting better. Many take their lives at this time because now they have the energy and initiative to do what they had only previously thought about doing.

6. Help the adolescent identify problems. Often the problems seem so many and so big that the individual feels overwhelmed. Feeling overwhelmed, he loses perspective and sees no way out. Helping the youth to identify and even list on paper the different problems allows the person to see them in a more manageable form.

7. Help the adolescent to identify the resources he has to handle the problems being faced. Here you are guiding the youth toward hope as he begins to see that not only may the problems be "bite'sized" but also that help is available.

Here, as well as throughout your conversations, help the youth to draw on the resources of faith and Scripture. This is a good point to quote or read some of the promises of God concerning God's love and His willingness to stand with us in times of trial.

Realize, however, that in spite of the fact that you may see great hope and can see how quickly this young person could move past this crisis with the right steps, the young person may be so mired in depression that he cannot see either the way out or even that there is a way. The only response you may get from him may be, "Yes, but. . . . " That can be frustrating to you; but you need to realize that if you keep getting this kind of resistance, the youth may not get out of his depression until he has intensive professional help or is on medication or even, in extreme cases, is hospitalized.

8. Get the youth to do something constructive to change things. If you can get the young person to agree to do something constructive, often that can start the ball rolling toward health and a resolution of the crisis. Again, however, don't think that just because things look better immediately the crisis is over. You will need to keep in touch with the youth and have others help you monitor what is happening.

9. Identify some people you or the young person will talk to about this situation. A good question to ask in many counseling situations is, "Who else knows about this?" If the youth says, "You are the only one who knows," you need to explain that you cannot bear the burden of being the only one who knows. And you cannot. This responsibility needs to be shared.

Try to get the young person to suggest some persons he will agree to talk with or that you may talk with. If he balks, press him; this is important. If he says he cannot think of anyone, then you suggest two or three persons. However, one of the advantages of having him name some persons is that you then will have clues about some important persons in his life who may be allies in this fight against suicide. For instance, if he insists that his parents not know, does that tell you something about those relationships?

All of this raises the issue of confidentiality. You cannot afford to run the risk of being the only person who knows about this suicidal crisis. If the youth steadfastly refuses to permit you to talk with someone, then in this situation you have the right and the responsibility to break the confidence and talk with a professional counselor, a pastor, an adult youth worker, or possibly the youth's parents. I would tell the youth what I was going to do. I would explain to the youth as carefully as I could that my talking with someone was not an act of betrayal. Rather, it is an act of love and concern.

Do you have any right not to talk with the youth's parents about this situation? Urge the young person to talk with them. If the youth says he will not and does not want you to tell his parents, I would not promise not to tell them. Instead, I would talk with the pastor and the counselor to whom I refer the youth and get their perspective on informing the parents. That way, I would not be alone in making that difficult decision. But, unfortunately, in some cases, if the parents knew, they would prevent the child from getting the needed help.

10. Deal with the method. If the young person has gone so far as to decide on a method of suicide, then he is probably tied to that particular method. Studies consistently show that suicidal persons become almost romantically attached to a particular method of suicide.

Therefore, one of the most important steps you can take in preventing the suicide of this youth is to ask him to allow you to keep "in safe keeping" the method of his suicide. We are talking here of the adolescent's giving you a gun, a rope, a razor, a bottle of pills, or some other means of suicide. You do not make or force him to give you the object. But if he will, it may be a big step toward safety.

11. Take some positive action to show the young person that something has been and will be accomplished because he came to talk to you. Talk about what you are willing to do to help him get past the crisis. Do not overpromise. Be realistic. This plan of action will include getting the youth further help, talking with some people who need to know, continuing periodic checkups with you, and possibly interviewing with the family in some way.

One step mentioned is getting the youth further help. To whom do you refer a suicidal youth?

• the family physician, if he is a wise and sensitive person who will do more than just prescribe some medication.

• a psychiatrist whose reputation is strong, not only as one who prescribes medication but also as one who is a good counselor.

• a pastoral counselor who is well trained and has experience in dealing with suicide.

• a clinical social worker with the same qualifications as above.

Your pastor should be a help to you in making this referral.

Should the person to whom you refer the youth be a Christian? By all means, if that is possible. However, in a suicidal crisis, I will refer to a non-Christian who ably handles suicidal persons before I will refer to an inexperienced or minimally competent Christian counselor or doctor.

To make the referral I suggest that you do the calling. Talking to a professional about personal crises is intimidating to adolescents. If you sense that this crisis is serious, call the professional with the youth in the office and briefly tell the professional the situation. When the appointment is set, you may offer to go with the youth but without being present in the session itself.

If the young person steadfastly refuses for a referral to be made, explain the danger of that decision. Explain that even if he chooses not to go you will be talking to a professional about the situation.

12. Make a suicide contract with the youth. After you have mapped out your strategy with the youth about what both of you are going to do to handle this situation, ask him to promise you not

to commit suicide. If he will not make the promise long-term, ask for a twenty-four- or forty-eight-hour contract.

Ask the youth to agree to this statement: "I will not intentionally or accidentally, now or in the future, take my life. If I begin to think seriously about doing so, I will talk with you." As you look the youth in the eye, ask, "Will you promise me that?" Make sure you get an affirmative response with eye contact.

Is that actually effective? Yes, almost always.

At this point your conversation is ending for now, but your strategy to deal with this crisis must be doggedly pursued.

End the time with prayer. Offer up to God some of the problems and concerns you have heard from the young person. Be specific as you ask for God's help. Mention by name some of those persons who will be assisting this young person to get through this crisis. Claim the promises of God and His power as you pray for the days ahead.

Before we talk about your post-talk strategy, let me mention some don'ts that relate to this whole process.

• Don't try to shock or dare the adolescent out of suicide. In other words, do not dare the person to go ahead and do it.

• Don't belittle or shame the youth for what he feels. Even though what he feels or why he feels that way may seem trivial or shameful to you, stifle your feelings and take him seriously.

• Don't try to argue the person out of suicide, and don't engage in a philosophical debate about suicide.

• Don't leave the person alone if you believe the risk of suicide is imminent.

Next, it is time to carry out the post-talk strategy.

1. If you have discovered the youth to be immediately suicidal and yet will not let you or others help him and will not even allow you to stay with him, as that young person leaves your office/ presence, call the police, his parents, and your pastor. The police will intervene if the danger is immediate.

Will this action hurt your relationship with the youth? Probably, for now. But saving a life is worth the risk of a damaged relationship.

2. If the young person has been open and cooperative and you have already contacted the counselor who will see the youth, begin to contact those persons whom you have mutually agreed need to know about what is happening. Try not to panic them,

but let them know that the situation is serious and that the main thing they can do is to keep in touch with the young person. As a pastor, I would definitely want to know what was going on at this point. For one thing, it helps tremendously for the pastor and youth minister to be colleagues together in this crisis.

3. Check back with the adolescent soon after your talk. Keep in close contact especially until the relationship with the counselor begins to solidify. Even then your contact needs to be regular.

What can you do to prevent youth suicide?

First, work with the parents of the youth to help them in their understanding of adolescence, of the specific tasks of parenting, and of special issues their children are facing. Include in this training several sessions on adolescent suicide with special attention to the major clues.

Second, train your youth workers to be knowledgeable, positive role models and motivators for the youth. This training should also include training in understanding adolescence and youth suicide.

Third, help your young people to understand what they are going through in adolescence and equip them through discipleship to cope with adolescence and to know how to grow in their faith.

I do not suggest doing suicide education with the youth. Suicide education with the youth, I believe, is less helpful in suicide prevention than is training parents and youth workers.

What should one do after an attempt has been made?

First, provide pastoral care to the youth and his family. Then, if the attempt is public information, call others together and try to interpret to them what happened and why. Emphasize the inadequacy of this way of dealing with problems. Coach the youth on how to respond to this young person when he returns to the group.

After a suicide has occurred, the pastoral care of the family is an obvious need. The grief after suicide is one of the most difficult griefs persons ever experience. And the grief almost never ends, although its intensity diminishes. A helpful book for you and for the family in this area is John Hewett's *After Suicide*.[12]

You can help others deal with their grief and some weeks later a teacher might plan a series of sessions on grief, or a pastor might deal with the subject in a sermon. Explain that this person chose death, but challenge others to choose life. Encourage them to promise one another that they will not choose suicide as a way to deal with their problems.

You might set up some opportunities for the youth to have a small-group discussion of what has happened and offer individual sessions with you or other knowledgeable people. Six months after the suicide, a youth leader could do a follow-up session to talk about the death and to determine how the youth are coping with that death.

In the summer of 1980, while at the Glorieta Baptist Conference Center in New Mexico, I received word that a close friend of mine had taken his life. Out of that experience I wrote this book. I know firsthand of many persons who were at the point of suicide who are now alive, because they read an earlier edition of this book. Why? Because someone helped them to see that there was a way out and that the option of suicide was not really an option.

I am convinced that many concerned Christians can be on the front line of defense against suicide. I am convinced that some are able to point the way out of a personal crisis and to help troubled persons close off that "option" of suicide. I am convinced that with the equipment of your faith, your compassion, and your knowledge, you are a formidable foe of youth suicide.

Looking Ahead

IN THE PREFACE OF this book, I asked you to go on a journey
of learning. That journey has taken you down some interesting
and some scary paths. But I hope from each path there has been
something learned. One path might have demonstrated the complexity of suicide, another an understanding of the thinking of a
suicidal person, and another a specific way to help that you perhaps had not thought of previously.

If you have read carefully, you may have confronted yourself in
the pages of this book. Somewhere an insight may have come into
your sense of life and death and the meaning of existence. Somewhere in these pages you may have recognized some of your own
motivations and probably some of your own struggles. This kind of
self-confrontation can be invaluable as you seek to become a gifted
helper of others. There are some issues in life that must be faced if
we are to understand how we can minister to others. I hope that you
know yourself better for having read this book.

Having read this book on suicide and its prevention, I must
warn you against one danger. If and when you become aware of a
suicidal crisis with a person, you may be tempted to "run back to
the book." You may say, "If I could only remember what that book
said to do now." I hope you will continue to find this volume a
continuing reference that you consult. But I also hope that in

a suicidal crisis you will "trust your gut." Trust your instincts about what needs to be done. Be guided by the Spirit of God about what needs to be said.

I mention this danger, because these pages contain many facts and many lists of points. In trying to deal with a suicidal person, you do need to be an informed helper, but you do not need to be tied up by handling that situation "just according to the book." Each situation is unique, and each helper will handle the situation differently. So let this book be your guide, not a fetter that binds you. Whatever else you do in helping a person on the brink of suicide, you need to be genuinely and spontaneously who you are as their family member or friend.

As I look back at all that has been discussed in this book, what would I say in summary? I suppose it comes down to an urgent plea to love others and especially to demonstrate that love when those around you are down and facing difficult times. This obviously should not be the only time we express love, but the expression of love is certainly needed at this time. Do not assume that others know of your love nor the depth of it. Say it and show it! The very act of reading this book has been an expression of love as you have sought to become a more informed helper in the battle against suicide.

There is one other word that needs to be said here. The focus of this book has been the individual who is suicidal and you as one of the suicide prevention helpers. I have taken a basically individualistic approach to dealing with the problem of suicide. That approach must be taken, but if we as a culture are to deal with suicide, there must also be a broader look at our society and the way it contributes to suicide.

In the United States, we permit a level of violence that few other nations would tolerate. Note the violence of much of our entertainment. Recognize the carnage of death on the highways that seems often to be passively accepted as just one of the costs of being a mobile people. Look again at the number of murders by handguns in the United States. Realize the massiveness of the child abuse problem. We are a violence-prone and therefore a death-haunted society. Until more and more people raise voices of protest against such violence, the efforts to halt its increase will be impotent. To deal with suicide, we must also deal with the culture in which suicide occurs.

There is one single issue in this picture of suicide that if addressed appropriately could significantly change the number of suicides in any one year. That issue is the control of handguns. As earlier noted, many suicidal persons become "married to" their chosen method of suicide. If access to that method can be limited, the number of suicides can be reduced.

Several years ago I attended a presentation by the medical examiner of Dallas County (Texas) in which he did a report on the suicides in that county in a one-year period. Repeatedly he noted in the evidence gathered at the scene of these suicides that persons who had used handguns had just purchased them. Obviously, they did so for the one purpose of ending their lives with them. How many of those suicides could have been avoided if immediate access to the means had been limited?

I talked with a mother whose young adult daughter had taken her life with a handgun. This young woman was doing her medical residency in a major hospital. Exhausted and despondent, she decided to end her life. It was evening and the gun stores were all closed. She found the phone number for a gunshop owner, called him, and talked him into opening his store so she could buy a handgun. After purchasing the gun, she went immediately to her apartment and shot herself. Would she be alive today and serving her patients if she had been denied immediate access to that handgun? Perhaps and perhaps not. But given the impulsiveness of many suicidal persons and their commitment to one method, isn't it worth the effort to limit the availability of this means that the majority of persons in the United States use to take their lives? I think it is.

Finally, since 1945, the world has been on a suicidal course with the nuclear arms buildup. We stand on the brink of the suicide of the human race. That the nations of the world can "play" with the notion of global suicide does not go unheeded by suicidal persons. To deal effectively with suicide, we must wage peace in a world that seems to be driven to war. Peace and the affirmation of the goodness of the gift of life must be held high and embraced boldly in a war-torn, death-bent world.

Can you help prevent a suicide? Yes. The task may be difficult, at times disappointing, and at times confusing. But it is no less desperately needed to be assumed by caring people. Suicide is a cry for help. If the cry comes to you, you can help.

Notes

Chapter 1

1. This list of "possible motivations for suicide" is a modified version of one included in a "Training Workshop Outline" by Marv Miller, Ph.D., Suicide Information Center, San Diego, CA, copyright 1982.
2. In Sylvia Plath, *The Collected Poems,* ed. Ted Hughes (New York: Harper & Row, 1981), p. 224.
3. Albert Camus, *The Fall* (New York: Vintage, 1956), p. 76.
4. Erwin Stengel, *Suicide and Attempted Suicide* (New York: Jason Aronson, 1974), p. 59.
5. Ibid., p. 60.
6. Ibid.

Chapter 2

1. Stengel, *Suicide and Attempted Suicide,* p. 145.
2. National Center for Health Statistics Monthly Vital Statistics Report, October 23, 1988.
3. World Health Organization, Geneva, Switzerland, *World Health Statistics,* annual. Reported in *World Eagle,* Wellesley, Massachusetts, September 1989, p. 28.
4. This list and some of the explanations of these groups are from a "Training Workshop Outline" by Marv Miller of the Suicide Information Center, San Diego, CA.

Chapter 3

1. Hans Selye, *Stress without Distress* (New York: New American Library, 1974).

2. David J. Klugman, Robert E. Litman, and Carl I. Wold, "Suicide: Answering the Cry for Help," *Social Work,* vol. 10, no. 4 (October 1965), p. 50.

3. Aaron T. Beck, Maria Kovacs, and Arlene Weissman, "Hopelessness and Suicidal Behavior," *Journal of the American Medical Association,* vol. 234, no. 11 (December 15, 1975), pp. 1146–49.

4. F. E. Crumley, "Adolescent Suicide," *Journal of the American Medical Association,* vol. 241 (1973), pp. 2402–7.

5. A. Alvarez, *The Savage God* (New York: Random House, 1972), p. 118.

6. Frank B. Minirth and Paul D. Meier, *Happiness Is a Choice* (Minneapolis: Baker Book House, 1978), p. 115.

7. Maggie Scarf, *Unfinished Business* (New York: Ballantine Books, 1980), p. 28.

8. Ibid., p. 42.

9. *The Journal of Nervous and Mental Disorders,* vol. 164, 1977, pp. 231–246.

10. *The Harvard Guide to Modern Psychiatry,* ed. Armand Nicholi, Jr. (Cambridge, MA: Harvard University Press, The Belknap Press, 1978), p. 220.

11. Arthur Henley, "Schizophrenia: Current Approaches to a Baffling Problem," New York: Public Affairs Pamphlet No. 460, p. 11.

12. Edwin S. Shneidman and Norman L. Farberow, eds., *Clues to Suicide* (New York: McGraw-Hill, 1957), p. 101.

13. Arthur H. Green, "Self-Destructive Behavior in Battered Children," *American Journal of Psychiatry,* vol. 135, no. 5 (May 1978), pp. 579–582.

14. Wayne E. Oates, *Nurturing Silence in the Noisy Heart* (Garden City, NY: Doubleday, 1979), p. 87.

15. Ibid., pp. 94–95.

16. Hawton et al, "Motivational Aspects of Deliberate Self-Poisoning in Adolescents," *British Journal of Psychiatry,* vol. 141, 1982, pp. 286–291. As reported in Shaw, et al, "Suicide in Children and Adolescents," *Advanced Pediatrics,* Vol. 34, 1987, p. 322.

17. "Note: Toward a Profile of the Older White Male Suicide," *The Gerontologist,* February, 1978, vol. 18, no. 1, pp. 80–82.

18. All of these verbal clues are listed by Louis Wekstein in *The Handbook of Suicidology* (New York: Brunner/Mazel, 1979), pp. 62–63.

19. These clues are a few of those listed in Marv Miller's "Training Workshop Outline."

Chapter 4

1. Wekstein, *Handbook of Suicidology,* p. 72.

2. Beck, A. T. et al, "Development of Suicidal Intent Scales" in *The Prediction of Suicide,* Beck, Resnick, and Lettieri (eds), (Springfield, Ill.: Charles C. Thomas Publisher, 1974).

3. Shaw, Kailie R. et al, "Suicide in Children and Adolescents," *Advanced Pediatrics,* vol. 34, 1987, p. 325.

4. Alvarez, *The Savage God,* p. 117.

5. Ibid.

6. Volunteer Manual, Suicide Prevention of Dallas, 1979 ed., pp. 106–7.

7. Shaffer, David, et al, "Preventing Teenage Suicide: A Critical Review," *Journal of American Academy of Child and Adolescent Psychiatry,* vol. 27, no. 6, November, 1988, p. 681.

8. Percy Knauth, "A Season in Hell," *Look,* January 18, 1972, p. 76.

9. Robert A. Caro, "The Years of Lyndon Johnson," *The Atlantic Monthly,* November 1981, p. 44.

10. Stout, Kate, "Marsha Norman: Writing for the 'Least of Our Brethren,'" *Saturday Review,* September–October, 1983, p. 31.

Chapter 5

1. Andre Haim, *Adolescent Suicide* (New York: International Universities Press, 1974), p. 142.

2. Daniel J. Levinson, et al., *The Seasons of a Man's Life* (New York: Ballantine Books, 1978), p. 219.

Chapter 6

1. Lowell R. Weitkamp, et al., "Depressive Disorders and HLA: A Gene on Chromosome 6 That Can Affect Behavior," *New England Journal of Medicine,* vol. 305, no. 22 (November 26, 1981), pp. 1301–6.

2. Tsuang, M. T. "Risk of Suicide in the Relatives of Schizophrenics, Manics, Depressives, and Controls," *Journal of Clinical Psychiatry,* 1983, vol. 43, pp. 396–400.

3. Schulsinger, F., Kety, S. S., Rosenthal, D. et al. "A Family of Affective Disorders" in *Origin, Prevention and Treatment of Affective Disorders,* ed. by M. Schou and E. Stromgren, London: Academic Press, 1979, pp. 277–289. Reported in "Epidemiology of Suicide" by Mary Monk in *Epidemiology Reviews,* 1987, vol. 9, pp. 51–69.

4. This is from another study conducted by Schulsinger and associates that is reported in "Generalizable Treatment Strategies for Suicidal Behavior" by Susan J. Blumenthal and David J. Kupfer, *Annals of the New York Academy of Sciences,* vol. 487, pp. 327–340, see especially p. 332.

5. Blumenthal and Kupfer, ibid.

6. Lois Wingerson, "Searching for Depression Genes," *Discover,* February 1982, pp. 60–64.

7. Monk, Mary. "Epidemiology of Suicide," *Epidemiologic Reviews,* vol. 9, 1987, pp. 51–69.

8. August Y. Napier, with Carl A. Whitaker, *The Family Crucible* (New York: Harper & Row, 1978), pp. 56–57.

Chapter 7

1. Karl Menninger, *The Vital Balance: the Life Process in Mental Health and Illness* (New York: Viking Press, 1963), p. 266.

2. H. H. Remmers and D. H. Radler, *The American Teenager* (New York: Bobbs-Merrill, 1957), pp. 31–38.

3. Herbert Hendin, *Suicide in America* (New York: W. W. Norton, 1982), p. 46.

4. Ibid., p. 40.

5. Joel Rebibo, "Teenage Suicide on the Rise," *The Jerusalem Post,* 18 January 1986, p. 16.

6. Max Day and Elvin V. Semrad, "Schizophrenic Reactions," *The Harvard Guide to Modern Psychiatry,* Armand M. Nicholi, Jr., ed. (Cambridge, MA: Belknap Press of Harvard Press, 1978), pp. 212–213.

7. Robert J. Lifton, personal remarks at the Texas Baptist Christian Life Commission's annual workshop, Fort Worth, Texas, 22 February 1983.

8. Jane E. Brody, "'Autoerotic Death' of Youths Causes Widening Concern," *New York Times,* 27 March 1984, C-1.

9. Hugh A. Storrow, quoted in Theodore Irwin, "Depression: Causes and Treatment," Public Affairs Pamphlet No. 488, p. 12.

10. "Teen Suicide," *People,* 18 February 1985, p. 85.

11. Frank B. Minirth and Paul D. Meier, *Happiness Is a Choice* (Minneapolis: Baker Book House, 1978), p. 115.

12. John H. Hewett, *After Suicide* (Philadelphia: Westminster, 1980).

Bibliography

Suicide Prevention and Intervention

Cappuzzi, Dave and Golden, Larry. *Preventing Adolescent Suicide* (Muncie, Indiana: Accelerated Development, Inc., Publishers, 1988). Written from a perspective of secular psychology, this is a comprehensive and helpful book.

Duckworth, Marion. *Why Teens Are Killing Themselves* (San Bernadino: Here's Life Publishers, 1987). A Christian's search and findings on the motivations behind teenage suicide and what the church can do to prevent those deaths.

Faberow, Norman L. *The Many Faces of Suicide: Indirect Self-Destructive Behavior* (New York: McGraw-Hill, 1980). From a pioneer in the suicide prevention field, this volume deals with less obvious forms of suicide that in some ways have become socially acceptable.

Hendin, Herbert. *Suicide in America* (New York: W. W. Norton and Co., 1982). This is a psychosocial approach which considers such factors as age, different social groups, violence, and alcoholism plus the case against suicide on secular and pragmatic grounds.

Maltsberger, John T. *Suicide Risk: The Formulation of Clinical Judgment* (New York: New York University Press, 1986). Written by a psychiatrist, this volume deals in depth with the assessment of suicide risk. Intended for professional counselors.

Merck Sharp and Dohme. The following booklets are available in multiples of 25 through North Wales Press, Inc., P. O. Box 1486,

153

North Wales, PA 19454 with checks made to Merck Sharp and Dohme:

Before It's Too Late (25 for $7.50)
Suicide in Young People (25 for $7.50)
Suicide—It Doesn't Have to Happen (25 for $7.50)
Suicide in Youth and What You Can Do About It—A Guide for School Personnel (25 for $7.50)
Suicide in Youth and What You Can Do About It—A Guide for Students (25 for $6.25)
Suicide Prevention in the Classroom: Curriculum Guide (25 for $12.00)
Suicide and How to Prevent It (25 for $9.25)

Quinnett, Paul G. *Suicide: The Forever Decision: A Book for Those Thinking about Suicide, and for Those Who Know, Love, or Counsel Them* (New York: Crossroads/Continuum Publishers, 1988). Designed for suicidal persons and for nonprofessionals who are seeking to help them.

Rosenthal, Howard. *Not with My Life You Don't: Preventing Your Suicide and That of Others* (Muncie, Indiana: Accelerated Development Inc., Publishers, 1988.) Written by a counselor in private practice, this is written in a light, breezy style for the person who is contemplating suicide or has a friend or family member who is.

Shneidman, Edwin. *Definition of Suicide* (New York: John Wiley and Sons, Inc., 1988). Both theoretical and practical, this book, written by one of the most noted American authorities on the subject, creates an intimate portrait of the suicidal person.

Sizemore, Finley H. *Suicide: The Signs and Solutions* (Wheaton, Illinois: Victor Books, 1988). Most of the same ground is covered as in other suicide prevention books, but the information is updated and the perspective is Christian.

Post Suicide Grief

Bolton, Iris and Mitchell, Curtis. *My Son, My Son* (Atlanta: Bolton Press, 1984). This is a guide to the grief experienced after a death or loss, including suicide. Reported by persons who have been through grief following a suicide to be very helpful and practical. (Available from Link Counseling Center, 218 Hildebrand Ave., Atlanta, GA 30328. Cost is $10.95 plus $2.00 postage.)

Dunne, Edward J., et al, editors *Suicide and Its Aftermath: Understanding and Counseling the Survivors* (New York: W. W. Norton & Co., 1987). Designed for professional counselors, this work includes research findings and treatment suggestions interspersed with the personal experiences of survivors.

Hewett, John. *After Suicide* (Philadelphia: Westminster Press, 1980). A survivor's manual by a clinically trained pastor written specifically for the family. Includes an excellent chapter on answering children's questions.

Lukas, Christopher and Seiden, Henry M. *Silent Grief: Living in the Wake of Suicide* (New York: Charles Scribner's Sons, 1988). A survivor and a psychologist write about the silence surrounding suicide and how survivors can heal and anyone can help them cope.

Ross, Eleanora "Betsy". *After Suicide: A Unique Process* (Iowa City, Iowa: Ray of Hope, Inc., 1980). This booklet offers insights and ideas which experience has shown to be helpful to grievers of a suicide death. Discusses the differences between "normal" and "after suicide" grief, what to tell children, ideas for personal help, how to help others, and "do's and don'ts" of listening.